# A Journey into Spiritual Growth

# A Journey into Spiritual Growth

## EVELYN CHRISTENSON

compiled by Sarah Peterson Hage

Chariot Victor Publishing
A Division of Cook Communications

Chariot Victor Publishing
A division of Cook Communications, Colorado Springs, Colorado 80918
Cook Communications, Paris, Ontario
Kingsway Communications, Eastbourne, England

This book contains adaptations from the following books by Evelyn Christenson: *Gaining through Losing, What Happens When We Pray for Our Families,* and *"Lord, Change Me!"*

Cover and Interior Design: Oh, Wow! Creative
Cover Illustration: Barbara Rhodes

**Library of Congress Cataloging-in-Publication Data**
Christenson, Evelyn.
A journey into spiritual growth/by Evelyn Christenson: compiled by Sarah Peterson Hage.
p.   cm.
ISBN 1-56476-765-5
1. Christian life.   2. Prayer--Christianity.   3. Christenson, Evelyn.
I. Hage, Sarah Peterson.   II. Title.
BV4501.2.C494      1999                          99-15578
248.4--dc21                                        CIP

1 2 3 4 5 6 7 8 9 10 Printing / Year 03  02  01 00  99

# CONTENTS

Gratefully dedicated to the three faithful women who, with great business expertise and deep spiritual insight, have been used by God to run my ministry since 1973— releasing me to write and to reach out to the world with Jesus' salvation and prayer's power:

Sally Hanson
Sue Hanson Moore
Diane Berggren

# INTRODUCTION

arah Peterson Hage once again has carefully and lovingly gleaned snapshots of my writings for this book. This new collection of short word pictures on a myriad of subjects is intended to take you on a spiritual growth journey with me. Some are from days past and some from just yesterday. But all are as fresh as God's faithfulness to us—which is new every morning.

Sarah's desire, and mine also, is that you will walk thoughtfully through some of them, skip for joy at others, and sometimes pause to reflect on what God is saying to you too. But we trust that always, as God speaks to your heart as He has to mine through His Word, you will hide the truths deep in your heart. And then you will find the victory of obeying, and the thrill of walking hand in hand with God—listening and talking to Him, your friend—and mine.

Thanks, Sarah!

When I was a little girl, my parents owned a greenhouse filled with blooming flowers. It was during the Depression, and when things got really difficult, we always knew where we could find my mother— standing praying in the calla lily bed. She was surrounded by tall, stately lilies, their pure white faces lifted toward heaven. Mother told me, "The calla lilies seem so pure and holy that I can almost feel them breathing up to God." So the calla lily became our family flower, reminding us of her prayers and ours.

# A New Process

*For whom He did foreknow, He also did predestinate
to be conformed to the image of His Son.*

Romans 8:29, KJV

 have discovered through the years that surprising things happen when I pray, "Lord, change me—don't change my husband, don't change my children, don't change my pastor, change *me!*" This doesn't mean that I approve or even condone everything they do, but rather that I concentrate on how *I* handle my actions and reactions. More and more the fact comes into focus that they, and not I, are responsible before God for their actions. But I am responsible for the changes that need to be made in me.

This concept became the process whereby I was to become more Christlike, conformed to His image, as stated in Romans 8:29, "For whom He did foreknow, He also did predestinate to be *conformed to the image of His Son.*" And since being Christlike is my goal, I must expect this process to continue throughout my life and end only "when He shall appear" and I shall be "like Him" (1 John 3:2).

Although it was to be 14 months before the "Lord,

change me" concept was to become an actuality, the process had started. God had launched me personally on a 14-month gestation period. The "birth" would not take place until over a year later. This was the process of facing the reality of *my* need to change—again and again and again.

The struggle was like a hot iron inside me. That's the only way I can describe it. And it took 14 solid months of turning to the only adequate, worthy Source of change—God Himself—and of searching His Word and allowing Him to make changes in my life, not in anybody else's.

"O God," I kept praying, "don't change anybody else, not my husband, not my children, just change ME!"

To this day, it is one of the most important prayers I ever prayed, and still pray almost daily.

*Dear Father, show me* my *need to change into the person you want me to be. Lord, keep me praying that prayer until the awesome day I see Jesus—and then am completely like Him. In His precious name, Amen.*

# WITHOUT A WORD (PART 1)

*Search me, O God, and know my heart; Try me and*
*know my anxious thoughts; And see if there be any*
*hurtful way in me, And lead me in the everlasting way.*
Psalm 139:23-24, NASB

ord, I will never speak again—never—if this is
the price my husband has to pay for my being
a public speaker." And I wept as I prayed, "Lord, I
want You to change me into the kind of wife You
want me to be."

Why was I telling God I would never speak again?
My personal agony was precipitated by what had
happened the week before at our denomination's
national conference, where I was reporting on the
six-month "What Happens When Women Pray"
experiment. Just before the banquet started, a man
carrying what looked like a movie camera arrived
and said to me, "Wave your arms and make believe
you're speaking." Then "Get animated," he chided.
As I complied, our national director, sitting at my
right, whispered laughingly out of the corner of her
mouth, "I think that's a TV camera!" And I was horrified to discover that she was right!

Early the next morning the jabs started—not at me,
but at my husband—from fellow pastors and friends.

"How does it feel to be the husband of Mrs. Christenson?" One pastor glanced at the shocking pink dress I was wearing and remarked to Chris, "I saw your wife on TV. Wow! It wasn't in technicolor, though." To my horror, the local TV station had chosen the segment showing my pseudospeech to represent our entire national conference on its news program. All week long Chris had borne the brunt of this cruel teasing. It became so embarrassing that I was the most crushed wife you could possibly imagine when we left the conference. I arrived home broken-hearted and puzzled.

God didn't take me up on my offer to give up my speaking and teaching, but He did begin that day to answer my prayer, "Lord, change me." He already had the next step in my spiritual maturity planned and ready for me. He started that morning to teach me a great principle which began a process in my life that is still at work.

*O Lord, please keep me searching Your Word*
*so You can keep searching my heart.*
*Show me every attitude, word, and action*
*displeasing to You. Please keep changing me,*
*Lord. In Jesus' precious name, Amen.*

## Without a Word (Part 2)

*So that . . . they may be won over without a word.*

1 Peter 3:1-2, NRSV

fter I began to pray for the Lord to change me, I discovered something new about myself— because my daughter told me!

At the dinner table one evening Jan, our just-turned-18 eldest, abruptly announced, "Mother, I don't ever want to hear your philosophy again. Do you know that the tone of your voice actually changes when you start giving your philosophy? I know what's coming every single time."

"*Me* again?" I pushed my chair from the table, flew up to my bedroom, and threw myself, sobbing, on my bed.

What was God teaching me this time? Jan always had been an independent first child, determinedly doing her own thing—following the encyclopedia's instructions for formal table setting while still in second grade; conquering the world of reading in sixth grade by winning our denomination's national reading contest. Her "I-can-do-it-myself,-Mother" personality had been there from birth, but always under

Mother's guidance. So what was happening to her now? What had legally becoming an adult at her eighteenth birthday done to her?

Then, agonizing in my soul, I prayed, "Lord, don't change Jan. I know she's a teenager who needs to find her way in the world. Just change me! Lord, make me the kind of mother You want me to be. O God, I know she's growing up. Show me, please, how You want me to change!"

Then began in earnest what was to stretch into 14 months of soul-searching for me.

As I looked in the Bible for direction, God gave me a principle from 1 Peter 3:1-2 that guided my "changing" and carried me through those difficult 14 months. At that time the emphasis for me from God was that others were to observe my chaste and reverent behavior. "So that . . . they may be won over *without a word*" (NRSV, italics added).

*Dear Lord, guide my actions and my talk, so that people will see You in all that I do. Keep teaching me that it is not what I say to and at people that will make them want to be like me, but my lifestyle with Jesus shining through my humble and obedient actions.*
*In Jesus' name, Amen.*

## Without a Word (Part 3)

*The wisdom of the prudent
is to give thought to their ways. . . .*
Proverbs 14:8, NIV

he principle from 1 Peter 3:1-2 (letting others observe chaste and reverent behavior without a word) was originally written regarding the husband-wife relationship. Yet I found that the "without-a-word" principle also worked with mother and a daughter becoming legally of age. I determined not to impose my philosophy on Jan again. No more "preachy" mother!

Keeping my advice to myself wasn't easy. Jan even enrolled at my alma mater as a freshman that fall! Oh, how I could have helped her by telling her just how to do everything. After all, hadn't I spent seven years with her daddy on that campus? And hadn't I, as secretary to the president, typed the disciplinary letters to parents and worked with the details of scholarships and college administration? But I restrained myself from offering my help. She didn't want it. Her independent attitude prevailed. She had to find out who she was—by herself.

I've learned since that that time wasn't easy for Jan

either. She has confided to me that frequently, those first few weeks, she would sit in her dorm, bite her lip, and blink hard to keep back the tears—determined to become independent—determined to make her own decisions in college. And at the same time I was sitting home just as determined—blinking back my tears—determined to let her find her own philosophy of life, to find her own way in the world.

When the first child turns 18 and decides to cut the apron strings, parents (especially mothers) almost bleed to death. Their wounds seem to be much deeper than those of the children, and heal so much more slowly. Letting go of Jan was one of the most devastating things that had ever happened to me. How I thank God for five years of preparation before our next child became of age. I didn't bleed nearly so much, for I had had five years to change my "smotherhood" to "motherhood." And Nancy could walk with much more confidence in the field which Jan had plowed as virgin soil those many years before.

*Dear Father, give me the wisdom to discern how I can best influence those close to me. Help me to change my smotherhood to the motherhood You desire in me. Teach me to let You be God in all my loved ones —not me. In Jesus' name, Amen.*

# WITHOUT A WORD (PART 4)

*And you yourself must be an example to them by doing good deeds of every kind. Let everything you do reflect your integrity and seriousness of your teaching.*
Titus 2:7, NLT

 he most surprising and thrilling thing to come out of those 14 agonizing months of keeping my mouth closed and letting God change me was a birthday card the next year from my Jan. It was signed: "To my mother—who says so much in her silence."

I had learned the first step in becoming more Christlike—*admitting* that I was the one who needed changing, and in silence *living* my life before others.

The struggle paid off in many ways, but one of the most gratifying was when Nancy, our middle child, came home from her part-time job four years later, burst into the living room and said, "Mother, I found you in the Bible! I was just reading my Bible and found you in Titus 2:7." Tears came to my eyes as she read it to me. "And you yourself must be an example to them by doing good deeds of every kind. Let everything you do reflect your integrity and seriousness of your teaching."

I cried in my heart, "O God, have I really lived in

front of Nancy an 'example . . . of good deeds . . . love of truth . . . and . . . in dead earnest'? Are there really those who are being won, not with my words but by observing me?"

*Dear Lord, thank You so much that the advice from You in Your Word, the Bible, does work. Keep me praying, "Lord, change me" every day. In Jesus' name, Amen.*

## LET HIM ASK OF GOD

*If any of you lack wisdom, he should ask God,*
*who gives generously to all without finding fault,*
*and it will be given to him.*
James 1:5, NIV

ord, I want to change. But how do I discover the 'chaste and reverent' behavior You require in 1 Peter 3:1-2? Especially since I've been trying so hard for so long? Is there more, Lord? How should I go about becoming what You want me to be now?"

When I asked God these questions, He showed me that He gives answers. All I needed to do was ask: "If any of you lack wisdom, he should ask God, who gives generously to all without finding fault, and it will be given to him" (James 1:5, NIV). One definition of wisdom is "that endowment of heart and mind which is needed for the right *conduct of life.*" Wisdom is not just philosophic speculation or intellectual knowledge, but a practical, applied lifestyle. It is not only knowing something in your head, but applying it to your life so that it becomes a part of you.

Over and over again during those 14 months, He reassured me that He wanted to give me all the wisdom I needed. The gift of wisdom is the only gift promised to all who ask for it. The other gifts are given by the three Persons of the Trinity as they please to distribute them.

In 1 Corinthians 12:8-11 we read that the Holy Spirit divides gifts to every man as He wills. Romans 12:3-6 shows us that "God hath dealt to every man the measure of faith . . . having then gifts differing according to the grace that is given to us." Then, in Ephesians 4:7 and 11, we read, "But unto every one of us is given grace according to the measure of the gift of Christ . . . and He gave some, apostles; some, prophets; and some, evangelists; and some, pastors and teachers." Thus Christ, too, gave people of differing gifts to the churches as He desired. But the gift of wisdom is different. Every believer can ask for, and receive, the precious gift of wisdom for making changes in his life.

*Dear Father, I don't know how to change into the person You want me to be. But thank You that You will give me wisdom every time I ask for it. In Jesus' name, Amen.*

# If Any Lack Wisdom

*Lead me in Thy truth, and teach me: for Thou art the*
*God of my salvation; on Thee do I wait all the day.*
Psalm 25:5, KJV

 had been given an assignment—to develop in four messages our denomination's women's annual theme, "God's Word for a New Age." I was to prove that the Bible was an adequate guide for this new age—an age of exploding knowledge, with technical libraries becoming obsolete every six months, and with a whole new world being conquered in outer space.

Trying to come up with the material for my messages, I drew a blank. Finally, I panicked, realizing I had only two months left to find the solution. So, I sought my green chair "prayer closet," fell on my knees, and begged God to give me the answer—but no answer came. In desperation I reached for my Bible, opened it to where I was reading devotionally, and started to read Psalm 25.

Suddenly one little word in the fifth verse almost jumped off the page at me. W-A-I-T. "Lead me in Thy truth, and teach me: for Thou art the God of my salvation; on Thee do I *wait* all the day" (italics added).

"O Lord," I cried, "I'll take You at Your Word. I'll trust You. I won't read any books on the subject. I'll just stay in *Your* Book and and let You tell me what I should teach those women."

Then every day for the next six weeks I read the Scriptures at random. And each time God stopped me (as He had at the word *wait*), I would jot down the specific thought on a separate piece of paper. When I finished this process, God had a surprise for me. I looked at the hopeless pile of random notes and announced to the family that I needed to use the dining room table to divide these into some semblance of order.

As I read through these disconnected, scattered thoughts gleaned from my Bible reading, I realized that they were logically dividing themselves into four specific subjects. With mounting enthusiasm and curiosity, I reread each grouping and discovered that these random notes fell into a natural outline form. In almost a state of shock I, who had always thought of myself as the "commentary kid," looked at the four piles of notes in outline form for the four messages which would prove that God's Word is an adequate guide for our sophisticated, proud minds. The Bible was alive—sufficient for our new age!

*Dear Lord, thank You that the Bible is a living book— able to answer all the questions in our lives. Keep me continuously discovering all the exciting answers You already have recorded for me. In Jesus' name, Amen.*

# READ UNTIL

*His delight is in the law of the LORD; and in His law doth he meditate day and night.*

Psalm 1:2, KJV

wo years after my "Lord, change me" plea, God offered me a new project. This time I was to let God *change me through His Word* while I kept my philosophy to myself. Most mothers go through a time of deep introspection when their children leave the nest. Now I had joined their ranks. I too reevaluated myself—soon to be out of a job just as I was becoming experienced at being a mother.

I set out in earnest using the process God had taught me, allowing Him to tell me how He wanted me to change. Staying in the Scripture for instruction, I would read only until He spoke. Then I would stop to pray about what He had said, analyze His reason for stopping me at that particular point, discover the need He knew I had, and then determine what I could do to change. I underlined hundreds of verses during those 14 months. Here are a few that were most meaningful to me.

As I read in the Psalms, day by day, God gave me the *source* of wisdom that would effect changes in my life. First, He gave me Psalm 1:2, "But his delight is in the law of the Lord; and in His law doth he meditate day and night." In the margin of my Bible by that verse I wrote: "24 hours" and "all undergraduates, no alumni." I was to meditate in His law day and night, and not consider myself as having graduated from God's school of learning and changing. There was still more for me to learn.

How I was to approach this process was shown to me in Psalm 25: "The meek will He guide in judgment; and the meek will He teach His way" (v. 9), and "What man is he that feareth the Lord? Him shall He teach in the way that He shall choose" (v. 12). Coming to God humbly and meekly, admitting that I needed to be changed, was a new, emerging thought to me in those days.

*Dear Father, teach me to come to You humbly and meekly. I want to be changed by You. You are the omniscient, all-wise God of the universe and I only a mere human being. Teach me to humbly come to Your Word so I can continuously delight in it— and You its author. In Jesus' name, Amen.*

## SEARCHING FOR WISDOM

*The fear of the LORD is the beginning of wisdom, and the knowledge of the Holy One is understanding.*
Proverbs 9:10, NIV

 s I continued my project to let God change me through His Word, I underlined heavily in my Bible *the promise of authoritative direction from God* for me in Psalm 32:8: "I will instruct thee and teach thee in the way which thou shalt go; I will guide thee with Mine eye." There was no question about it, God was going to instruct me and He was going to guide me in my quest for instruction as to how I was to change.

As I read until God spoke from the Book of Proverbs during those 14 months, He gave me much instruction about obtaining wisdom: "yea, if thou criest after knowledge, and liftest up thy voice for understanding; if you seekest her as silver, and searchest for her as for hid treasures; then shalt thou understand the fear of the LORD, and find the knowledge of God. For the LORD giveth wisdom; out of His mouth cometh knowledge and under-standing" (Prov. 2:3-6, italics mine).

Then as God spoke to me forcefully out of the 139th Psalm, the idea of Scripture being profitable for reproof (2 Tim. 3:16) became evident. "Search me, O God, and know my heart; try me, and know my thoughts; and see if there be any wicked way in me, and lead me in the way everlasing" (vv. 23-24). God had to show me through His Word what displeased Him and what needed to be changed in me. In the margin I penciled, "Prayer: 'Lord, change me.'" Once again God was impressing upon me the truth that "the fear of the LORD is the beginning of wisdom" (Prov. 9:10).

*Dear Lord, You are looking into my heart and seeing all the things that displease You. Keep showing them to me in Your Word, the Bible, so I can be changed by You. In Jesus' name, Amen.*

# TRANSFORMED—
## BY THE RENEWING OF YOUR MIND

*But be not conformed to this world: but be ye*
*transformed by the renewing of your mind, that*
*ye may prove what is that good, and acceptable,*
*and perfect, will of God.*

Romans 12:2, KJV

As I searched the Scriptures, some specific points on how I could change began emerging during those 14 months. I remember rising early in the morning in a Fort Lauderdale condominium, struggling with what God meant when He had given me Romans 12:2 the month before: "But be not conformed to this world: but be ye *transformed* by the renewing of your mind, that ye may prove what is that good, and acceptable, and perfect, will of God" (italics added).

On December 29, 1969, I wrote in the margin of my Bible, "Transformed—same original word as Christ's transfiguration." Did God want me changed as dramatically as Christ was on the Mount of Transfiguration when His face shone as the sun and His raiment was white as the light? Then I wrote, "Changed—from worm to butterfly." I almost felt like the surprised worm I had seen on a poster. Watching a butterfly soar overhead, the worm was saying, "Who, me change?"

Then I wrote in the margin of my Bible beside Romans 12:2, "Pronouns—does God want *me*?" The pronouns were so very, very personal. I circled them. No mistaking it. God wasn't talking to my husband, my children—but to me. Then the abrupt note in my Bible said, "Spiritual maturity—period." Yes, that's what all that changing was about—to be mature in Him. Like Him. Proving what is His good and acceptable and perfect will—for me.

*Dear Father in Heaven, so many things I do and am are so much like the non-Christian world around me. Please change me every day, making me more and more like my Jesus. In His precious name, Amen.*

# How to Change

*. . . being confident of this, that he who began
a good work in you will carry it on
to completion until the day of Christ Jesus.*

Philippians 1:6, NIV

od continued to show me how to change through my 14-month "Lord, change me" process. I read Galatians 2:20: "I am crucified with Christ; nevertheless I live; yet not I, but Christ liveth in me; and the life which I now live in the flesh I live by the faith of the Son of God, who loved me, and gave himself for me." Then, in my Bible, I wrote, "Ego moves to the side—Christ center of me." The *how* to change was becoming obvious. I was to let Christ live in me, transforming me into the likeness of Himself.

There were many specific instructions, but Philippians 2:3, with the notation, "Humility—April, 1969," was so meaningful to me at that time: "Let nothing be done through strife or vainglory; but in lowliness of mind let each esteem other better than themselves."

God showed me some affirmation of the learning in silence through my 11-year-old Kurt as we were reading together that January. "Isn't it amazing how much you can learn when you don't argue?" he commented on Philippians 2:14: "Do all things without murmurings and disputings." Renewing of my mind!

God seemed to reassure me through one verse of Scripture in my struggle to become changed, more Christlike. In February I had a heavy speaking schedule and was utterly exhausted at a retreat in Mount Hermon, California. I fervently prayed for God to change me before the Saturday night banquet. Two days later, after an almost miraculous rejuvenation for the banquet, I marked this in my Bible: ". . . being confident of this, that he who began a good work in you will carry it on to completion until the day of Christ Jesus" (Phil. 1:6, NIV).

A verse I would only be able to understand later prompted me to write "me" in the margin beside it. Like Paul, would I be a more effective servant of Jesus after this? Would my ministry for Christ be more effective because of the experiences of these 14 months? "But I would ye should understand, brethren, that the things which happened unto *me* have fallen out rather unto the furtherance of the Gospel" (Phil. 1:12, italics added).

*Dear Lord, thank You for the good work You have begun in me. Thanks, too, that little by little You let us see that these changes really are for the furthering of the Gospel. In Jesus' name, Amen.*

# Changed—
## Through My Spiritual Diary

*Your word is a lamp to my feet and a light for my path.*
Psalm 119:105, NIV

ecently I did a project in preparation for an assigned retreat theme of "God's Living Word." To prove to myself—and those at the retreat—that the Bible had been alive in my own life, I dug out the three Bibles from which I had read devotionally since I was 18 years old. I went through those Bibles, systematically and laboriously, and recorded in three columns (one for each Bible) the most significant underlined, and usually dated, Scriptures. As I pored over these three Bibles for a month I had a surprise. I could tell from the passage I had underlined whether I had been in victory or defeat, joy or depression, death, birth, surgery, ill ness, open doors, challenge, or closed doors—a spir itual diary of my life from the time I was 18! As th evidence piled up, I slowly began to realize that Go had always given *specific answers for specific needs specific times.*

For example, I was quite shaken when past wife accused me publicly of leaving out a theol

cally important point in a message. Checking the tape of the message later, and finding that I really had said it, didn't ease the embarrassment. But God had the answer for me. The next morning as I read Psalm 19 one word stood out in the 14th verse— "Thy." "Let the words of my mouth, and meditation of my heart, be acceptable in Thy sight, O Lord, my strength, and my Redeemer."

In the margin of the Bible I wrote, "In Thy sight, not in people's sight." And then I prayed, asking the Lord to remove all the negative thoughts I had had the night before. I asked Him to forgive me and "make EVERY thought and ALL my words acceptable to YOU, LORD!" Immediately I sensed His affirmation, His OK on that message. The desire to defend my innocence melted. God had changed me!

*Dear Lord, I know I'm a people pleaser. But please burn deeply in my heart that You are the One I must please. Change all my reactions and attitudes until I completely please You. In Jesus' name, Amen.*

# His Joy

*But let all those who put their trust in Thee rejoice; let them ever shout for joy, because Thou defendest them; let them also that love Thy name be joyful in Thee.*

Psalm 5:11, KJV

t was pouring rain as I started for an out-of-state retreat. Three miles from home a truck, a compact car, and Evelyn stopped for a red light, but the car behind me didn't. Crunch. And all four vehicles accordioned into one. I recovered from the jolt to my back but evidently not from the jolt to my nervous system, for as I drove during the following week I kept my eyes as much on the rearview mirror as I did on the road ahead of me!

The next weekend I was to drive to a northern Minnesota retreat. I couldn't. I felt nothing but apprehension and fear at the possibility of being hit from behind. And the theme for the retreat was to be J-O-Y!

Just before I was to drive to the retreat, God gave the answer as I was reading in the Psalms. A smile spread over my face as I read: "But let all those who put their trust in Thee rejoice; let them ever shout for joy, because Thou defendest them; let them also that love Thy name be joyful in Thee" (Ps. 5:11). Immediately I saw my problem—failing to trust

Him! At that moment He exchanged my fear for *His*—yes, literally—His joy. The apprehension disappeared, and I drove, a changed woman, to that J-O-Y retreat, really experiencing what I was to preach.

My spiritual barometer for years has been 1 John 1:4: "These things [are written] that your joy may be full." I can always measure the amount of time I'm spending in the Scriptures by how much joy (not superficial happiness, but deep-down abiding joy) I have. When I find a lack of joy in my life, the first thing I check is how much time I'm spending in God's Word!

*O God, keep me alert to my lack of real joy—especially during my life's hard times. Then infuse me with Your joy as I return to the precious written words from You to me. In Jesus' name, Amen.*

# Trusting God with Health (Part 1)

*O God, Thou art my God; early will I seek Thee: my*
*soul thirsteth for Thee, my flesh longeth for Thee in a*
*dry and thirsty land, where no water is.*

Psalm 63:2, KJV

'm convinced that God has a sense of humor.
One year our church experienced a great mov-
ing of God, and every Sunday for four months I had
the privilege of praying with at least one, and frequently with many, who came to find Christ as their
Savior. It was exciting.

Suddenly I had pain in my middle and was hospi-
talized for tests. A "No Water" sign was hung on the
end of my bed, and by early morning the real or
imagined desperation for water had set in. In my dis-
comfort I prayed, "God, please give me something to
read in my Bible that's just for me, right now." Psalm
63 popped into my head, although I didn't have the
foggiest idea what it was about. I grabbed my Bible,
turned to the Psalm, and read: "O God, Thou art my
God; early will I seek Thee." So far so good. It was
5:30 in the morning.

As I read on in that first verse, I cried, "Lord, is this
a joke?" "My soul thirsteth for Thee, my flesh longeth

for Thee in a dry and thirsty land, where no water is."

Then I saw in verse 2 what God was really trying to say to me: "To see Thy power and Thy glory, so as I have seen Thee in the sanctuary." God showed me that my real problem was not the lack of water, but in not wanting to miss seeing Him move in the sanctuary. My real rebellion was at being put on a shelf in the midst of the action!

*Dear Lord, being useless on a shelf is so hard. Please make me content in You—and let You change me through those waiting times. In Jesus' name, Amen.*

# Trusting God with Health (Part 2)

*I beseech you therefore, brethren, by the mercies of God,
that ye present your bodies a living sacrifice, holy,
acceptable unto God, which is your reasonable service.*
Romans 12:1, KJV

hen my medical tests were over I remember smiling bravely as my doctor told me that I would have to have surgery right away. After he left, I burst into tears. Reaching for my Bible, I prayed, "O God, give me something for right now!" Immediately Romans 12:1 flashed into my mind, "I beseech you therefore, brethren, by the mercies of God, that ye present your bodies a living sacrifice, holy, acceptable unto God, which is your reasonable service."

Now I had His answer. I had given Him so completely my spirit—my mind, my emotions, my energy. All that I was, I thought. But *I had never given Him my body!*

Surgery and days of recuperation came and went, but I was still kicking at being left on a shelf when so much was going on in "the sanctuary" at our church. Not until the next Sunday when I tuned into a pastor friend's radio program did I obey God's instruction to me. I gave God my body—once and for all.

Gradually my attitude toward my health changed. Illness didn't disappear completely, but my attitude toward it changed. I relaxed. I felt somewhat like the pastor who called his banker saying *our* car is in the ditch. Through the years I have learned to say, "God, our body is sick."

God changed me from an overprotective guardian of my body to one who entrusts that body to Him. What a great way to live! Whenever I don't feel well, I just say, "Lord, if You want me to be well enough to do the job for You that's coming up, thank You. But if not, just teach me what You have for me to learn while I'm on a shelf." This obedience to His specific instruction has done more than anything else in my life to take the pressure off and change my whole outlook on life.

*Lord, people around me seem so preoccupied with their bodies. What a precious privilege to be able to entrust mine completely to You—for Your care and Your use. In Jesus' name, Amen.*

## GOD OUR CREATOR

*. . . the earth is full of the goodness of the LORD. By the word of the LORD were the heavens made; and all the host of them by the breath of his mouth.*

Psalm 33:5-6, KJV

ne of the favorite things we do during our vacation in Michigan in August is to lie on the beach at midnight and watch the fantastic display of shooting stars. The summer our Kurt was seven I read an article in the *Reader's Digest* about a father who got his seven-year-old boy up in the middle of the night to see the shooting stars because, he reasoned, there were some things more important than sleep. So, when the exhibition was at its peak, we decided it was time for Kurt to join the rest of the family on the beach. The excitement and the "ohs" and "ahs" mounted with each display of God's celestial fireworks.

But the real excitement came the next morning when, as a family, we read at the breakfast table Psalm 33, and especially the fifth to ninth verses: ". . . the earth is full of the goodness of the Lord. By the word of the Lord were the heavens made; and all the host of them by the breath of his mouth . . . Let all the inhabitants of the world stand in awe of him, for he spake, and it was done." I found myself not only excited over an astronomical wonder, but changed into a mother awed at God's timing and selection of our daily reading—overawed that He wanted to tell us that He only had to speak and all this was done!

*O God, You are the magnificent Creator! Thank You for revealing this to us not only in the wonders we can behold, but in Your words written so many years ago— yet specifically for specific times for us.*
*In Jesus' name, Amen.*

## LIVING AND ACTIVE

*For the word of God is living and active and sharper than any two-edged sword. . . .*
Hebrews 4:12a, NASB

he beach at Lake Michigan is my favorite place to read God's Word and let Him speak to me. Every day while we are on vacation I rise early and, weather permitting, take my Bible down to the edge of the lake and read until He speaks. One morning I read such a great psalm about our God that I found myself skipping down the beach instead of doing my usual hiking. God had changed an ordinary, run-of-the-mill vacation day into one of exhilaration and exploding joy, joy that could not be contained in ordinary steps. The thrill that sent my body soaring like the eagle's blurt out in impromptu songs of praise as I adored Him for who He is and praised Him for what He is. Changed by a psalm? Yes, changed!

Fifty-nine years of underlining answers for actual situations have proven to me that the Bible truly is a *living* Book. "For the Word of God is living and active," Hebrews 4:12 (NASB) tells us. Yes, it is alive. It has answers in the midst of our knowledge explosion today—or tomorrow—on this planet and in outer space. And precept upon precept as I let it renew my mind, my attitudes, and wisdom to live by, I am changed. Changed into what is His perfect will for me to be.

*Dear Father, I stand in awe at how currently alive and active the Bible is in my life. You always know what I need, and use this alive book to change me right then. In Jesus' name, Amen.*

# HIDDEN TREASURE

*My purpose is that they may be encouraged in heart
and united in love, so that they may have the full
riches of complete understanding, in order that they
may know the mystery of God, namely, Christ, in
whom are hidden all the treasures of
wisdom and knowledge.*

Colossians 2:2-3, KJV

 was going to speak at a retreat on the subject
of "God's Living Word." I packed my three
Bibles and headed for the plane in Minneapolis,
where the security guard started systematically to
check my carry-on luggage. When he pulled out the
first Bible he gave me a "that's-a-nice-lady" smile.
The second one produced a puzzled expression on
his face. But, at finding the third, he was sure I had
hidden something valuable in those Bibles, and pro-
ceeded to search each one diligently. He even held
one up by its binding and shook it vigorously.

That guard never discovered the treasure I had hidden in those three Bibles. The omniscient Lord Jesus
Christ, "in whom are hid all the treasures of wisdom
and knowledge" (Col. 2:3, NIV), had given it to me.
Underlined and marked on those pages was all the
direction I had needed for a "chaste and reverent"
lifestyle since I was 18 years old. Line upon line, pre-

cept upon precept, God had taught me how to change.

When I have needed direction for my life, has He ever left me groping in the dark, trying to find my way? Oh, no! He has given me His Word as a "lamp unto my feet, and a light unto my path" (Ps. 119:105). And, as I have obeyed His instructions, He has changed me, step by step, into the person He wants me to be.

*O Lord, please don't let me ever forget the treasure I personally have from the Lord Jesus Christ. Help me to cherish it and obey Him as He makes me more and more like Himself. In His precious name, Amen.*

# Lord, Change Me for Others Too

*Your statutes are wonderful; therefore I obey them.*
*The unfolding of your words gives light;*
*it gives understanding to the simple.*
Psalm 119:129-130, NIV

Suddenly, the months of searching Scripture "without a word" were over. The "Lord, change me" gestation period came to an end. What had been a very private experience in my own life erupted, unplanned, at a retreat in Minnesota. Unannounced, it became a principle to be shared with others.

No, I hadn't changed the retreat theme. I had diligently prepared my messages on the theme those 800 women had chosen for their retreat—but God had other ideas.

While I spoke, one illustration from a previous women's retreat triggered the change of theme. I told these women that two years earlier, right after I had found such exciting answers when I had read only the Bible, I decided to try the wait process on the 400 women attending a retreat in Washington. Having no idea of what God was going to say to them, I sent those women out to read Colossians 3 by themselves. I had instructed them to read only *until* God spoke, and then to stop and pray about what He was saying to them.

In addition to speaking at that Washington retreat, I told them, I had also served as a counselor. A steady stream of women came to me for advice. I knew I didn't have professional answers for those women, so every time one came to me I listened to her problem and then asked the question: "And where did God stop you in your reading of Colossians 3 today?"

Do you know what happened? *In every instance* the Lord stopped each one of them at the answer to her problem. I didn't have to offer a single solution, because the Lord did. In fact, on Saturday night the retreat committee said to me, "God is doing such a great thing, let's not structure the Sunday morning service. Let's just ask the women to share what God has been saying to them out of the Scripture."

That Sunday morning for one-and-a-half hours the women shared what God had said. I was so overwhelmed that I finally asked them all to jot down on a piece of paper what God showed them when He stopped them in Colossians. I went home with a large manila envelope bulging with specific answers—not from me but from God.

*Dear Father, it is beyond human comprehension that You can know the thoughts and intents of each person's heart in a room; and then, as they read some Bible passage, You give them the exact answer they need. Holy Father, increase my faith! In Jesus' name, Amen.*

## FORGIVE AS HE FORGAVE

*Forbearing one another, and forgiving one another,*
*if any man have a quarrel against any;*
*even as Christ forgave you, so also do ye.*
Colossians 3:13, KJV

t one retreat, a very angry and distraught woman burst into my room as I was hurriedly throwing things into my suitcase to catch a plane for Minneapolis. I explained that I really didn't have time to talk with her, but she told me to keep packing while she talked. She trembled with anger as she ranted on about a woman she couldn't stand, a woman who was also attending the retreat. "Why," she exploded, "she actually talks and gossips about our pastor. And I won't go to prayer meeting if she's going to be there because I get so furious when she prays. Would you believe she actually prays against him right in front of him?

As she raved on, I paused in my packing, turned to her and asked, "And where did God stop you in Colossians 3?"

"In verse 13."

"What does it say?"

"It says, 'Forbearing one another, and forgiving one another, if any man have a quarrel against any;

even as Christ forgave you, so also do ye.'"

"Is that where He stopped you?" (Nod.) "How long have you been a Christian?"

"Three months."

"Did Christ forgive anything in you when you became a Christian?"

A look of shock crossed her face. Then she put her head on my shoulder and began to weep. "Oh, it's *my* fault, isn't it? I'm the one who needs to change, not her. I'm the one God needs to change." She had seen that she was to forgive others as He had forgiven her—forgiven her of all her past sins when she accepted Him as her Savior three months before.

I went to the airport with a wet shoulder, but left behind a woman who had learned to forgive as Christ had forgiven her—because God had shown her what was wrong with herself, not with the other woman.

*O Lord, forgive me when I see everybody else as wrong except me. Help me to realize that I need to forgive others in the incredible way You forgave me when I accepted You as my Savior.*
*In Your name, Jesus, Amen.*

## Restoration through Forgiveness

*You must make allowance for each other's faults and*
*forgive the person who offends you. Remember, the*
*Lord forgave you, so you must forgive others.*
Colossians 3:13, NLT

t a retreat, someone slipped a note to me:
"Please come to our cabin. We have a problem." I tucked the note in my Bible, promising myself
to see about the need after the service.

When I entered the cabin, I was sure I had never
felt a colder atmosphere. All the women were sitting
there in sullen silence with their chins slightly jutted
and arms crossed.

I soon discovered that they were all from the same
small town where their church had recently split.
Half of them had stayed in the church and the other
half had left. At home they weren't speaking to one
another. But the unknowing camp registrar had put
them all in the same cabin!

And there they sat—each one blaming the other.
My first suggestion was that they read Colossians 3.
They refused! One lady was sitting right beside me,
holding her Bible. I asked her several times to read
Colossians 3:13 for us, but she stubbornly repeated,
"No, I won't."

A couple of hours passed, but I was getting nowhere. They finally agreed on one point: the problem in their town was all the fault of one man—*he* did this, and *he* did that. And if *he* hadn't done that, we wouldn't have done that. "Yes," they all agreed, "it is all his fault because our church broke up."

"He sounds like a pretty horrible guy, and I guess it is probably all his fault—or at least most of it is. But," I said," do you think one percent of the blame might be in this room?"

From the far corner a woman said hesitantly, in a barely audible voice, "I think there's one percent over here."

Then someone else said, "I think maybe there's, ah, ten percent here."

Finally the woman with the Bible looked at me and stammered, "I-I think I can read Colossians 3:13 now." And slowly she read: "You must make allowance for each other's faults and forgive the person who offends you. Remember, the Lord forgave you, so you must forgive others" (NLT).

At a quarter to one in the morning, we finally ended the encounter with our arms around each other, weeping and praying. And those women prayed only one prayer, "Oh, Lord, don't change that guy back home. *Change me!*"

*Dear Father in heaven, please help me not to drive divisions in the body of Christ because I think only they are wrong. Show me the sin of my attitude—and then the joy of restored relationships when I forgive. In Jesus' name, Amen.*

## ANOTHER SURPRISE

*. . . that they may all be one; even as Thou, Father, art in Me, and I in Thee, that they also may be in Us; that the world may believe that Thou didst send Me.*

John 17:21, NASB

arly in the morning our doorbell rang and there stood a man my husband had counseled many times. He had been married, divorced, and remarried to the same woman. And his life was still a mess. "Could I see the pastor?" he asked.

My mother-hen defense for Chris went up and I said, "It's terribly early and Chris is still asleep. Could you come a bit later?"

"I have to tell somebody. Could I tell you?"

Monday morning! But I said, "OK. Tell me."

He said, "Do you know what? The most amazing thing happened to me. A week ago I was driving my truck, blaming everybody for what was going on in my home—my kids, my wife, my employer. But suddenly the Lord said to me, 'You are the one who needs to be changed, not all the rest of the people.' As I drove I prayed, 'Lord, change *me.*'"

I sat there in amazement: *Lord, change me!*

"I have had the most marvelous experience," he

continued. "I went home, and there was that wife that I had married, divorced, and remarried. We were having such a rough time. And the next morning when I woke up there she was, the same wife. But I loved her with a love I didn't know was possible. I took her in my arms and said, 'Oh, honey, how I love you.' It was just great.

"Now, I hadn't really spoken to my dad for many years. I went out to see my old dad who had been an invalid for a long time. I went to his bedside and said, "Dad, I just came here for one reason. I came here to tell you I love you.' And the tears started to trickle down his face as he took my hand and said, 'Sonny, I have waited since you were that high (measuring three feet from the floor with his hand) to hear you say that.'

"Mrs. Chris, I had to tell somebody, because all I've been praying is 'Lord, change me.' *And all of these things have happened in my whole relationship with people—just because I prayed 'Lord, change me!'*"

I suddenly realized that God had not given this fabulous thought to me to be kept selfishly to myself—only to see myself change. But He had intended all along that it was to be shared with others whom He also wanted to change.

*O God, in every broken relationship, bring to my mind that powerful, life-changing little prayer: "Lord, change me." Use it to restore the unity of our family and church family members—so the world will see our oneness in You and Jesus. In Jesus' name, Amen.*

# WRITE GOD A LETTER

*Do not merely listen to the word,*
*and so deceive yourselves. Do what it says.*
James 1:22, NIV

requently at our retreats, after God has spoken to us through His Word, we write Him a letter. We tell Him what we will change in our lives because of what He has pointed out to us. After having each one seal her letter to God in a self-addressed envelope, I collect the letters and keep them for about a month. Then I put them in the mail so the writer can check up on herself to see if she really *did change*—or if she forgot and went on in the same old condition.

I always "read until" with the others at retreats, and here is one letter I wrote:

"Dear God: You told me that I am hung up on not really accepting 'that person' back into the fellowship of the beloved, and that I am to restore that person who was overtaken in a fault—lest I, Evelyn, should be tempted like that—even though I don't think that is one of my weaknesses. I will restore that person in every possible way. Lord, open doors, make me comfortable around that person again."

The very next day God honored my prayer, and arranged a surprise breakfast meeting. I keep that letter as a constant reminder of how I had to change in my attitude toward one who had slipped—of how God had told *me* to change and I had obeyed.

The changes come, however, not when God speaks but when we *obey* what He has told us. We are changed only when we *apply* to our lives what He has said.

*Dear Lord, help me never to forget that the Bible says it is my responsibility to initiate reconciliation. My intentions frequently are no good, Lord; forgive me for deceiving myself by not actually doing what I told You I would. In Jesus' name, Amen.*

# CHANGED—
## WHEN I STUDY GOD'S WORD

*All Scripture is inspired by God and profitable for teaching,*
*for reproof, for correction, for training in righteousness. . . .*
2 Timothy 3:16, NASB

hould I let God change me through devotional reading or Bible study?" That is not a fair
question, because *both* are essential for a well round-
ed, transformed life. Devotional reading is never a
substitute for deep, systematic Bible study—but it is
a complement to it. And the Lord does change me
*when I study His word.*

Paul gave Timothy excellent advice when he said,
"Study to show thyself approved unto God" (2 Tim.
2:15). He also counseled him to: "Remember that
from early childhood you have been familiar with
the sacred writings which have power to make you
wise and lead you to salvation through faith in Jesus
Christ. Every inspired Scripture has its use for *teaching*
the truth and *refuting* error, or for *reformation of the*
*manners and discipline in right living,* so that the man
who belongs to God may be efficient and equipped
for good work of every kind" (2 Tim. 3:15-16, NEB,
italics mine).

I'm so grateful that God did not ask me to give up

teaching when I prayed that He would make me the kind of wife He wanted me to be, for He would have deprived me of great joy. Digging into the Bible always produces a joy and an excitement that *changes* me into a different person. My spiritual barometer, 1 John 1:4, applies here, "These things are written that your joy [might] be full." Even if I'm willing to be changed by what God is teaching me, the end result is always joy. Deep Bible study also produces spiritual maturity—Christlikeness—in me.

One of the guidelines we gave to each participant of one of our neighborhood Bible studies was this: "The purpose of this study is for us to find our lifestyle out of God's Word. This will include accurately observing what the Bible really says and applying it to our daily lives. This reading is not intended to be an in-depth guide on how to study the Bible. Its purpose is to show how life-changing a thorough study of God's Word can be."

*Dear God, thank You for the exhilarating privilege of studying Your Word. Keep me diligent in accurately observing and studying so I will be changed by the Bible's teaching, reproof, correction, and training in righteousness. In Jesus' name, Amen.*

# PRE-STUDY PRAYER

*Blessed are those who hunger*
*and thirst for righteousness, for they will be filled.*
Matthew 5:6, NIV

s I study God's Word, approximately one third of the study time is spent in prayer. This prayertime is divided into four categories: before the study, while observing what the Scripture really says, while interpreting what it means, and when applying it to myself or those whom I'm teaching.

Just approaching my study time in prayer changes me. First, I pray about my personal preparation. Praying for *cleansing* before starting to study establishes a clear communication with God. Then expressing in prayer the hunger and thirst after righteous that I feel in my heart assures me of "God's filling" (Matt. 5:6).

Next, it is important for me to pray, *"Lord, remove all preconceived ideas* about this portion of Scripture I am about to study." It is always possible that something I have heard or studied previously has not been correct. Praying for God to remove all preconceived ideas (for the study time) willl enable Him to reveal fresh insights to me. I let my spirit soar as I thrill at new thoughts from His Word!

I also pray that God will *take control* of the study time so that all observations, interpretations, and applications will be truth. I must acknowledge my dependence upon Him if I want accurate, powerful, life-changing lessons for myself or those I will be teaching.

Then, *I ask God to be my Teacher,* inviting the Holy Spirit to be operative in me as I study. In John 14:26 Jesus said that the Holy Spirit would "teach you all things." Also, Paul prayed for the Christians at Ephesus that God would give them "the Spirit of wisdom and revelation in the knowledge of Him, the eyes of [their] understanding being enlightened" (Eph. 1:17-18). The Bible is more than a textbook of poetry, history, psychology, law, and letters; it is a living, personal message from God's heart to our hearts! And studying it thoroughly, deeply, and systematically produces *changed* people.

A good Bible study always includes three elements: *observation, interpretation,* and *application.* And as I diligently practice each part, *God changes me.*

*O God, I acknowledge I only will be changed when I actually live what I have observed and studied in the Bible. Forgive me for thinking that accumulating head knowledge is sufficient. In Jesus' name, Amen.*

# CHANGED—
## WHEN THE HOLY SPIRIT REMINDS

*These things have I spoken unto you, being yet present with you. But the Comforter, who is the Holy Spirit, whom the Father will send in My name, He shall teach you all things and bring all things to your remembrance, whatever I have said unto you.*
John 14:25-26, KJV

any times God wants to change me not when I'm reading or studying His Word, or when I'm with a group "reading until He speaks." But when I find myself in a situation where I need help immediately without a Bible in hand, then the Holy Spirit brings to my mind the Scripture that meets my need at that moment. One of the primary reasons for reading and studying the Bible is to provide Him with the Word to bring to remembrance—*when we need it.*

Jesus said: "These things have I spoken unto you, being yet present with you. But the Comforter, who is the Holy Spirit, whom the Father will send in my name, he shall teach you all things and bring all things to your remembrance, whatever I have said unto you" (John 14:25-26).

Now, some of the disciples would be recording the words of Jesus in some of the books of the New

Testament. What a word of assurance this must have been for them. But was this promise of the Spirit's prompting given only to Peter, John, Matthew, and the other disciples who were with Jesus at that time? I think not. Prisoners of war and others who have had Bibles taken from them tell fantastic stories of the Holy Spirit recalling for them the Scripture they had learned previously. This is one of the most powerful ways God has used the Scriptures down through the ages. When there was a need, the Holy Spirit pulled from memory exactly the portion of Scripture that fit the need.

*Dear Lord, thank You that through the years the Holy Spirit has brought to my remembrance just exactly what I needed while I wasn't actually reading the Bible. Keep me hiding Your Word in my heart so it will be there to be recalled. In Jesus' name, Amen.*

# THAT I MIGHT NOT SIN

*. . . your Father knows what you need before you ask him.*
Matthew 6:8, NIV

view with awe my neighbor across our cul-de-sac who is working on the world's largest computer. My mind is boggled as he tells of the huge amount of words it can work on at a time and the billions of facts its memory banks can store. But we as human beings possess the world's most sophisticated and complex memory banks—our minds—and they store up all the information acquired by us from infancy.

The psalmist says: "Thy Word have I hid in mine heart, that I might not sin against Thee" (Ps. 119:11). This is the process of tucking the Word of God deep down in our hearts by study and memorization. As we read the Bible, study it, and listen to sermons from it, we are not to dismiss what God says to us, but are to *hide* those spiritual truths in the deepest recesses of our hearts, like spiritual computers.

When I recognize there is something wrong in my life that I know God wants to change, I feed the problem into the "computer" of my heart. Then, when I ask God to give me a solution, the Holy Spirit, the supernatural computer operator, often reminds me of a portion of Scripture—a verse or a single word—that shows me the specific sin that is causing my problems. Many times He flashes back: "pride" (Rom. 12:3) or "worry" (Phil. 4:6).

Occasionally, before I'm even aware that something is wrong, or before I know there is a problem to feed into my heart's "computer," the Holy Spirit is already spelling out an answer to me. He knows the need or the problem before I ask, before I consciously formulate it into words.

Jesus said in Matthew 6:8 that our Heavenly Father knows what things we have need of *before* we ask Him, and the solution is recalled from my memory bank before I spell out my need. That's even less time than this largest computer in the world takes to summon answers! Yes, before I even realize my sin, the Holy Spirit is reminding, prodding, reproving with His gentle nudge or stating in no uncertain voice, "That's SIN!"

*Dear Holy Spirit, thank You that You are the divine member of the Godhead who operates my mind's memory book. Help me to be willing to listen and admit I need to change when You recall this awesome wisdom for me. In Jesus' name, Amen.*

# BE HOLY

*. . . be ye holy; for I am holy.*
1 Peter 1:16, KJV

y Spiritual Operator, the Holy Spirit, has a favorite reminder He spells out for me: "B-E Y-E H-O-L-Y; F-O-R I A-M H-O-L-Y" (1 Peter 1:16).

I hid this verse in my heart many years ago, and I'm surprised it isn't worn out from God's flashing it at me so often. But it gets to me every time. I immediately see my God high and lifted up, *holy*—perfect attitudes, actions, and reactions. And what I've stored in my memory bank from His Word comes clicking back to me. And I know how holy God is— and how holy I'm expected to be! Recalled—to keep me from sinning.

I remember one day while on vacation at our cottage I had a sudden eye-contact with a man. I flushed slightly, enjoying his obvious approval of me. The next morning I asked God to enlighten my understanding of the sin of this type of encounter. Slowly, as if on a screen in my mind, the words "Be ye holy; for I am holy" came forward until they were in focus. I asked God for complete cleansing, and immediately I was *changed*. Communing with God as He gave me several pieces of wisdom for my next book, I was suddenly engulfed with adoration of Him. Welling up from the depths of my being, flowing into every inch of my body was the prayer, "O God, how good is vacation! Time to drink deeply of Your Word, to read good Christian books. Time to adore You rather than working under the tyranny of the urgent." Changed when the Holy Spirit recalled His "old faithful" verse.

*Dear Father, there is so much evil and questionable input from the world constantly bombarding my mind. Keep the Holy Spirit recalling that word HOLY every time I'm not alert enough to catch the danger by myself. I want to be holy like You!*
*In Jesus' sinless name, Amen.*

# NUMBER ONE RECALL

*And we know that all things work together for good
to them that love God, to them who are the called
according to his purpose.*
Romans 8:28, KJV

 omans 8:28 is the number-one verse the Holy Spirit recalls for me. In fact, He has reminded me of it so often that I have adopted it as my philosophy of life: "And we know that all things work together for good to them that love God, to them who are the called according to his purpose." God gave that verse to me at the time I lost my third pregnancy during our college days. He must have known then how my whole life would revolve around that verse—though I certainly didn't know it at the time.

I used to have to struggle to find the "good" in the seeming calamities of my life, but sooner or later I was able to see what God was doing and why He was doing it. And more and more through the years I am able to see the "why" of circumstances as soon as the Holy Spirit says, "Romans 8:28." What used to take time to figure out, now seems to come almost immediately and automatically.

And it works 100 percent of the time. When something especially bad happens, the Holy Spirit persists, "*All* things." It was hard at first, but as the years have come and gone, it has become easier. it's a matter of faith. As faith is exercised, it grows stronger and stronger. The faith is in the God of that verse— the One who is working out all things for my good. And the Holy Spirit is really recalling not a verse, but all that God has worked out for me for 54 years.

One of the greatest ways God changes me is by bringing Scripture to mind I have hidden deep in my heart. And He always picks the right Scripture at the right time. What a reason for staying in His Word daily—reading, studying, devouring it. And then what a challenge to stay so sensitive to the Holy Spirit's speaking that He can reach down and recall just exactly what I need at the very minute I need it!

*Dear Heavenly Father, thank You that, through the years, You have proven to me these weren't just empty words. As the Holy Spirit has recalled it perhaps thousands of times by now, it has actually become my philosophy of life. In Jesus' name, Amen.*

## EXCHANGED:
## STRENGTH FOR WEAKNESS

*Without faith it is impossible to please him; for he that
cometh to God must believe that he is, and that he is a
rewarder of them that diligently seek him.*

Hebrews 11:6, KJV

rayer is another way God changes me. When
I ask Him to change me, He actually
exchanges my sin or shortcoming for His perfect
attribute.

Often we ask God to change us, but then don't wait
for Him to answer our prayer. A secret I learned
many years ago is that God gives me some things
only when I wait.

Recently in a series of hectic days I had an unusu-
ally strenuous one. I drove to Wisconsin for an all-
day prayer seminar, lectured for six hours, and then
drove back home to Minnesota. I had just one-half
hour to cook my dinner, eat, and get back on the road
for another two-and-a-half hour lecture. At bedtime,
Chris, knowing my rigorous schedule, called me
from his travels in Florida. "Just wanted to know
how you made it through the day, Honey. How was
it?"

"Oh, Chris, all I can say is that it was another miracle. By the time I had driven home from Wisconsin I was so exhausted that I could hardly raise my arms, my stomach was hurting, and it was hard to think straight. But—when I started to speak at Bethel College tonight, I suddenly felt as fresh as if I had eight hours of sound sleep!"

What had happened? Before the evening seminar I took a few minutes to lie down and pray these words: "O God, exchange my exhaustion for Your strength." God had miraculously reached down, lifted my exhaustion, and then replaced it with His strength.

When we are fatigued, our tendency is to keep pushing and pushing, slower and slower, until we get the job done. But God's formula is so simple, and it takes such a short time to stop, ask, and wait for His answer.

However, there is a key to this formula: Ask, and then wait expectantly. This requires *faith*—not in the few minutes I might have in which to rest, but in the One who is to provide the strength. Hebrews 11:6 explains it so clearly: "But without faith it is impossible to please him; for he that cometh to God must believe that he is, and that he is a rewarder of them that diligently seek him." It is God who *exchanges* my fatigue for His strength. And He does it when I stop, ask in faith, and wait expectantly.

*Dear Father, this exchanging in my body defies all human laws. O God, I am so grateful for all those times You have performed this miracle for me. In Jesus' name, Amen.*

## EXCHANGED:
## THE MIND OF CHRIST FOR MY FALLIBILITY

*Your attitude should be the same as that of Christ
Jesus: Who, being in very nature God, did not
consider equality with God something to be grasped,
but made himself nothing, taking the very nature of a
servant, being made in human likeness.*

Philippians 2:5-7, NIV

he day before I started a large prayer seminar,
my son-in-law phoned and said, "Do you
want to hear a funny story?"

"Sure," I replied.

"Well, Jan and I were being entertained in a couple's home, and our hostess mentioned Pastor
Lyndon Karo. 'How do you know him?' Jan asked in
surprise. 'Oh, I read about him in a book on prayer.'
'My mother wrote that book,' said Jan. 'Oh,' said our
hostess as she glanced nervously around her house,
'if I had known, I would have cleaned my house better.'"

After Skip and I stopped laughing, he continued.
"Then our hostess became quiet. Then she blurted
out, *'I feel as if I'm entertaining God.'*" And at that Skip
and I roared with laughter.

But when I hung up the phone, God said to me—
*pride!* I pled with God to give me the mind of Christ.

"O God, please forgive me for that terrible attitude. I'm sorry. Please give me the mind of Christ." Immediately God brought Philippians 2 to my mind. "Let this mind be in you, which was also in Christ Jesus; who, being in the form of God, thought it not robbery to be equal with God; but made Himself of no reputation, and took upon Him the form of a servant" (vv. 5-7).

I was overwhelmed. Jesus was God (John 1:1). Jan wasn't God. I wasn't God—but Jesus, who actually was God, came to earth *as a servant.* My mind flashed to Mark 10:45 where Christ said He "came not to be ministered unto, but to minister." This was the "mind of Christ" I was admonished to have in me—the mind Jesus had when He came to earth from heaven.

"O Lord," I cried, "make me *only a servant.* Please give me the mind of Christ." Immediately God answered. Flooding over me was an overwhelming sense of only being a servant. The next morning when I started my seminar and looked out over all those people, I had the beautiful sense of being completely *their servant*—nothing more.

Pride over a funny story could have ruined the whole seminar, but God took that story and gave me what He really wanted me (and every Christian) to have—the mind of Christ. The mind of a Servant!

*Dear Father in heaven, thank You that Your Son, Jesus, my example, came to earth as a servant. Please exchange my sinful pride for His mind of servanthood every time I see myself as anything more than that. In Jesus' name, Amen.*

## Exchanged: God for Money

*For where your treasure is, there will your heart be also.*
Matthew 6:21, KJV

any years ago Chris and I made a promise to God that we would never ask a fee for my speaking. Even in the early days of my prayer seminars when love offerings rarely covered expenses and prayer-letter mailings, we simply trusted God. Somehow I had always felt He would withdraw His blessings if I started serving Him for the money I might receive.

After my first book came out and my cassette tape sales increased, I was still completely detached from the income. Then people started ordering the tapes by mail. And gradually I became more and more eager to see how many orders the mailman brought.

One day as I was returning from a seminar, speeding to get home as fast as possible to see how many orders had come, God said clearly to me, "Evelyn, that attitude toward money is sin!" I was horrified. I slowed the car down and cried, "Please remove all of these thoughts and this attitude right now, Lord. O God, forgive me. O Lord, change me! Please, please

You remove this from me." And in one sweep of His mighty cleansing hand, it was gone!

That night God had something to say to me out of His Word. As I was reading my Bible a phrase in Matthew 6:24 almost jumped off the page at me: "You cannot serve both God and money" (NIV). For three nights I found myself peculiarly drawn to that same verse. It was as if I wanted God to press it deeper and deeper into my being. "I cannot serve both God and money!" Why not? God gave me that answer in the same chapter when Jesus was warning us against laying up for ourselves treasures upon earth and telling us to lay them up in heaven. Then Jesus gave the "why": "For where your treasure is, there will your heart be also" (Matt. 6:21).

God didn't say that I never could be paid for my ministry. In fact, He has some explicit instructions about the workman being worthy of his hire; but the problem lay in *where my heart was*. And He *exchanged* my wrong attitude about money for His perfect one.

*Dear Lord, thank You for changing my attitude for Your attitude toward money. Forgive me for the times when I look to money for security rather than You. O God, how good it is to be banking in heaven for eternity instead of down here temporarily.*
*In Jesus' name, Amen.*

# Exchanged:
## Meekness for Self-Assertion

*. . . a meek and quiet spirit,*
*which is in the sight of God of great price.*
1 Peter 3:4, KJV

ometimes it's a little risky to ask God to change me. I remember a pastor at a World Day of Prayer speaking on the topic, "Be careful what you pray for—God may answer your prayer." And I learned the truth of this years ago when I asked God to give me a meek and quiet spirit.

While preparing a banquet message on God-like characteristics in women, I was pricked by 1 Peter 3:4, where it says that we should be adorned, not with outward hairdos, ornaments, and clothes, but with "a meek and quiet spirit." Recognizing something to be desired in my steamroller personality, I prayed for five consecutive days, "Dear God, please give me a meek and quiet spirit." This was the prayer on my lips and in my heart.

I must have thought God was going to "sugar coat" me by some supernatural process, for I was completely unprepared for the method He used.

At that time, our sixth-grade daughter had a divorced male teacher who liked to take his female pupils to a wooded retreat for outdoor education. When I refused to let our daughter go to the woods with him alone, he was furious, and came to tell me so. When I answered my doorbell, I saw him standing there with his face ashen in anger. And for the next half hour he raved and ranted at me for ruining his reputation in the community by not allowing my daughter to be alone with him in the woods, etc., etc., etc.! When he finally walked out the door, I had what I had prayed for—a meek and quiet spirit!

Yes, God had *exchanged* my personality trait for the one of His choice when I had asked Him to. But, oh, the process!

*Heavenly Father, give me the courage to keep asking You to make exchanges in my personality and lifestyle. I trust You, dear omniscient Lord, because I know You never make a mistake. In Jesus' name, Amen.*

## ADMITTING OUR BURDENS TO OTHERS

*Bear one another's burdens,*
*and thus fulfill the law of Christ.*
Galatians 6:2, NASB

hen I ask others to pray for me, they take my burden to God in prayer, and He makes the necessary changes—with awesome results.

Many of our heaviest burdens are completely hidden to those who would pray for us—unless we share them. How can we fulfill the law of Christ in all its potential if we refuse to admit our burdens to one another?

In order to benefit to the fullest from the prayers of others, we must *admit* our needs to them. In our prayer closets it is often difficult to confess our needs to God, but we find it almost impossible to admit a weakness or need to fellow Christians. However, this is a must if we expect to experience all the prayer support they are willing to give us.

When we first started our experimental praying, we all had a lesson to learn about praying for one another. One of our committee members had been taught to keep to herself her own needs and the needs in her family, an attitude she found almost impossible to change. She was a terrific pray-er, but she could not admit that *she* had a need.

One day she had to leave our meeting early because of a severe migraine headache. She knew that medication and rest would take several days to alleviate the problem. And she was having a baby shower at her house that night! As the time for the shower drew near, she found herself completely incapacitated. In desperation she finally decided to do what she never had done in her life: "O God," she prayed, "if You want somebody to pray for me, just have them call on the phone. I won't call anyone, but if this is what You want, tell them to call me."

Almost immediately three women called her, one after another. "Hi. Just wondering if there is anything I could do for you tonight," each one said. Stunned, she broke the inhibitions that had been binding her and not once but three times said: "Please pray for me. I don't feel well. I need you to pray for me."

Admitting she had a need was hard, but God honored her honesty and humility. By the time the guests arrived, there wasn't a sign of her migraine headache or nausea. Changed!

*Dear Father, please forgive all the times I have been too proud to ask for people to pray for me—and missed what You were waiting to do for me. Thanks for all those who hear my burdens with their prayer. In Jesus' name, Amen.*

## DEPENDENCE ON OTHERS

*Pray in the Spirit on all occasions with all kinds of prayers
and requests. With this in mind, be alert and always keep on
praying for all the saints. Pray also for me. . . .*
Ephesians 6:18-19, NIV

erhaps one of the reasons we find admitting
our needs to other people so difficult is that by
doing so we are admitting we are dependent—
dependent upon God and upon other people. We are
a generation of "I-can-do-it-myself-God" Christians.

Whether we want to admit it or not, we are dependent on other pray-ers. In Matthew 9:38 Jesus said,
"Pray ye, therefore, the Lord of the harvest, that he
will send forth laborers into His harvest." Am I a
laborer because someone, some time, some place,
obeyed Jesus' command and prayed that God would
sent forth a laborer to the field in which I'm working?
This is a humbling thought, and removes all the ego
and pride about *my* ministry, *my* calling. Because
somebody prayed, did I CHANGE into God's laborer?

If Paul was dependent on his friends to pray for
utterance to be given to him, how much of *my* having
utterance in my ministry is because somebody, or
many people prayed for me? In Ephesians 6:18-19

Paul asked prayer for utterance for himself and all saints—me! How much did I CHANGE because of them?

Frequently we don't know we have been depending on the prayers of others until we see the results. When Peter was in prison (Acts 12:5-19), he may not have been aware that "prayer was made without ceasing of the church unto God for him" (v. 5). Perhaps not until the chains fell off his hands, and he walked out of prison as the iron gate opened, did he realize that God must be answering prayer. Or was it when the believers finally opened the door of the house and he saw them "praying without ceasing," that he realized why he was freed?

When we experience relief from some physical problem before it runs its natural course, it may well be that our fellow Christians are obeying the admonition in James to "pray one for another that ye may be healed" (5:16). When we are miraculously *changed* physically, how dependent were we on God's faithful pray-ers?

How much do I change because other people pray for me? Only eternity will tell. Only God knows who activates the process of change that takes place in me.

*Dear Lord, thanks for all the wonderful people who faithfully pray for me. Lord, I know the power is not in the pray-er, but in You—the all-powerful One who answers their prayers! Thanks, Lord.*
*In Jesus' name, Amen.*

## Spiritual Warfare

*But I have prayed for thee, that thy faith fail not: and*
*when thou art converted, strengthen thy brethren.*
Luke 22:32, KJV

ince the Father and the Son are one, I'm constantly amazed that God had need of Jesus' prayers on behalf of others. Jesus must have known that this is the process God uses, yes, expects, when others have needs, for in His high-priestly prayer He prayed for His followers and for us.

And in that prayer Jesus prayed that the Father would keep them and us "from the evil one" (John 17:15). He didn't pray that God would remove us from the evil one's domain, Planet Earth; just that God would deliver us from him. Because Christ is our example in all things, we too should pray this prayer for other believers.

Jesus also practiced this kind of prayer specifically when Satan wanted to sift Peter. He said, "But I have prayed for thee, that thy faith fail not" (Luke 22:32). But in spite of Jesus' prayer for him, cocky Peter—cocksure he wouldn't fall into the enemy's trap before the cock would crow—denied his Lord. Jesus knew the importance of praying for those who are tempted by Satan.

In Ephesians 6:18-19 Paul's exhortation to pray always for all saints and for himself is part of the armor that Christians are to use in the battle against spiritual wickedness—the realm of Satan. In 1972 I bravely tackled a Bible study subject of "Ephesians in the Light of the Spirit World" (fools rush in where angels fear to tread), and experienced unusual resistance from the enemy. But in the margin of my Bible next to Ephesians 6:18 I wrote: "2/29/72. Great power first Bible study. Host of people praying. I could *feel* power. Never felt more when speaking." I had *changed* from an intimidated and harassed woman trying to prepare a Bible study that was a threat to Satan—*changed* into an empowered teacher. Because they prayed!

*Dear Father God, much of the time I don't immediately*
*recognize the source of trials in my life—*
*but You do. God, when people pray for me, You know*
*how to send victory over the cause—Satan.*
*In Jesus' victorious name, Amen.*

# Somebody Needs Me

*I urge, then, first of all, that requests, prayers,
intercession and thanksgiving be made for everyone. . . .*
1 Timothy 2:1, NIV

nherent in each human being is the need to be needed. It gives us a sense of self-worth, a zest for life, and a reason for living.

Corrie ten Boom told me that when she was five years old and had just received Christ as her Savior, her mother said to her, "Corrie, now you are an intercessor." And she found that the people living around her home needed her prayers. What a great way for a little child to find her self-worth.

Trying to motivate and instill a sense of self-worth in teenagers at a prayer seminar proved to be a difficult experience. There were 200 members of a confirmation class who, along with a church full of adults, were learning to pray. But their presence was not voluntary, and the paper wads, bubble gum, and paper airplanes displayed on the first night showed me what they thought of themselves as pray-ers.

At the second session one of them came to me and said she had a prayer request. "My ten-year-old sister cannot hear," she said. Fearing I'd never be able to motivate them if God chose to answer some way other than healing her sister, I decided on a plan. I challenged those 200 teenagers by giving them the request. I told them it was *their* responsibility, *theirs* to do whatever they chose with it. I held my breath all that next week waiting for the outcome. At the next session my fears proved to be in vain. I found myself surrounded by a whole gang of the girl's teenage friends as she excitedly announced, "Guess what happend to my sister? She can now hear without her hearing aid!" Those 200 teenagers had found the worth of themselves to someone in need.

After the last session of the prayer seminar, the pastor's wife came to me with tears in her eyes. "Do you remember the boy who was throwing paper airplanes and shooting paper wads that first night? (How could I forget him?) Do you know what he just prayed in our little group? He prayed, 'Dear God, please teach my dad what You've just taught me!" Oh, yes, we change when we discover we are needed.

*Dear Lord, thank You for teaching us that the most ordinary people, young and old, are used by You to bring the needs of other people to You. Thank You that when You answer their prayers, You have given them incredible self-worth. In Jesus' name, Amen.*

# God Needs Me

*You do not have because you do not ask.*
James 4:2b, NASB

ome of the greatest untapped potentials in our churches are our infirmed members. Many of them were great spiritual giants while their bodies were still strong, but now that disease or old age has forced them to become inactive for God as they are confined to their rocking chairs, wheelchairs, or beds, their spirits often become as shriveled as their bodies.

But I've discovered something exciting in our prayer seminars. Relatives and friends frequently bring these people to a seminar, and occasionally they even come by bus from nursing homes. I challenge these infirmed Christians that God *still* needs them, and I tell them that they can once again exercise as much and perhaps more spiritual power than they did before. I love to watch these bypassed citizens of God's kingdom unfold like a rose as they rediscover that God needs them.

One of our outstanding primary department teachers became physically unable to teach her class. Home-baked cookies and deep personal concern for every pupil had made her a teacher who was deeply loved. But after having to relinquish her class, she launched a new project from her hospital bed and home confinement—she spent the Sunday School hour praying by name for each pupil in her department and for the teachers and the superintendent. Almost immediately the other teachers began to report that amazing changes were taking place in that department. Discipline problems went almost to zero. Did God need her more in that capacity than teaching her class of primary boys and girls? Evidently. Yes, God had allowed her to be changed from an active to an inactive person, but instead of folding up in her confinement, she was changed into a powerful intercessor.

The startling discovery that God is using us does change our sense of self-worth. We are changed—needed—people. And that makes us joyful people!

*Dear Father, thank You that our need-to-be-needed is incredibly fulfilled by Your needing us. You can do everything without us, omnipotent Holy Father; but it is so wonderful that You let us help You run Planet Earth—through our praying! In Jesus' name, Amen.*

## SWEET AND BITTER WATER

*Doth a fountain send forth at the same place sweet
water and bitter? Can the fig tree, my brethren, bear
olive berries? either a vine, figs? So can no fountain
yield both salt water and fresh.*

James 3:11-12, KJV

hen I pray for other people, I find the truth of
James 3:11-12 becoming evident in my life. I
find it is impossible for two attitudes to be in me at
the same time. "Doth a fountain send forth at the
same place sweet water and bitter? Can the fig tree,
my brethren, bear olive berries? either a vine, figs? So
can no fountain yield both salt water and fresh."

When I pray for others, it takes my mind off my
complaints. There is always someone worse off than
me, and when I go into deep intercessory prayer for
that person I change from a self-centered complainer
into a person with genuine concern and love for that
one for whom I pray. Somehow I can't concentrate on
myself and pray out of love for others at the same
time.

I find, too, that it is impossible to pray for and gossip about a person at the same time. One of the great
results of a telephone prayer chain is that the prayers stop gossiping about other people's troubles

when they start praying about them. Also, "roast pastor" is no longer a Sunday dinner main dish when we really start praying for him.

I can't thank God for all the good things about a person and be filled with accusations at the same time. Somehow those two diametrically opposed attitudes can't be expressed simultaneously. This is one of the subtle results of thanking God for all our acquaintances—especially our enemies. During the process, we change.

I also find it impossible to pray for and be angry with a person at the same time. Could Christ have had something more in mind than the persons for whom He commanded us to pray, when He said in Matthew 5:44, "Pray for them which despitefully use you"? Could one of the results of praying for those who despitefully use us be that we, the pray-ers, are changed as we pray for them? But in order to effect this change, our prayers must be genuine. We cannot utter a few sweet words in prayer while the bitterness remains deep down inside. No, real prayer is the overflow of the heart.

*Dear God, whenever I start to criticize, find fault, or gossip about people, please remind me that Your solution is so simple—just sincerely pray for them. Thanks for changing me, not necessarily them. In Jesus' name, Amen.*

# MY SENSUAL SELF

*Such "wisdom" does not come down from heaven but
is earthly, unspiritual, of the devil.*
James 3:15, NIV

 ow that we've looked into the methods God
uses to change us, the haunting question arises: How can I be absolutely sure it is God who is
changing me? How can I know that my lifestyle, the
sum total of all my wisdom put into action, is really
from Him?

God showed me the fact that the Book of James
mentions four sources of wisdom from which I can
obtain knowledge that will change me. These four
are constantly vying for my lifestyle, but only one of
them is God. Only one of the four is a trustworthy
source of direction for the changes in my life

Is there any way, then, that I can test the source of
wisdom that is producing my lifestyle? James says
the proof is in *what it produces:* "The wisdom that
comes from heaven is first of all pure; then peace-
loving, considerate, submissive, full of mercy and
good fruit, impartial and sincere" (3:17). This is in
contrast to what the other three sources produce:
"But if you harbor bitter envy and selfish ambition in

your hearts, do not boast about it or deny the truth. Such "wisdom" does not come down from heaven but is earthly [from other people], unspiritual [from within our sensual selves], of the devil [from demons]. For where you have envy and selfish ambition, there you find disorder and every evil practice" (James 3:14-16, NIV).

Sometimes it is difficult to discern which source of wisdom has produced a change in me, because it is possible for sources other than God to produce temporary satisfaction with the good life, but the end result in me will always be the opposite of what God wants to produce in me. Superficial happiness may be produced from one of the other sources of wisdom, but there will be an absence of real joy and peace down deep within me.

*Dear Father, open my eyes to the fact all wisdom is not good and from You. Help me to discern when it is from one of the other three sources, and to refuse to obey their leading. In Jesus' victorious name, Amen.*

# I THINK

*Sanctify them by the truth; your word is truth.*
John 17:17, NIV

hat I think really isn't very impressive according to God's Word. There is only one Truth, and that is God Himself. And the only absolute truth on which we can depend for the right kind of changes in our lives is found only in God's Word (John 17:17).

We have a rule about this at our house. Last summer I overheard two of our children discussing it: "Mother always said truth is truth. It doesn't matter if you believe it or not. And not believing it has nothing to do with the fact that it is truth, and it will not change from being truth just because we choose not to believe it."

Yes, whether or not I agree with something has nothing to do with whether or not it is true. My "I think" about a subject neither negates it nor insures its being true.

But we are so prone to believe our "I thinks" are very important. Many times what is billed as a Bible study turns out to be an exchange of our "I thinks."

We read the Scripture portion and, using it as a springboard, dive immediately into the inner pool of "I thinks" and begin a discussion of whatever comes to our minds. When we are finished telling what we think about the subject, other class members usually retain what they think, and I keep what I think. It may have been a great discussion, but no one acquired any new truth.

A rule for Bible study that assures us of getting wisdom from the only worthy Source, God Himself, is that we don't discuss anything that is not answered in the portion of Scripture being studied on a given day. The teacher, and hopefully the pupils, will have studied the actual meaning of the text, and the answers no longer will be the participants' "I think" but God's Word. Then we know that the changes we make in our lives based on that lesson are not from the "I thinks" of people but from God Himself.

*Dear Lord, forgive me for ever believing what my fleshly side thinks is true. It certainly isn't a safe guide for my life. O God, keep me in Your Word so I can always be changing Your way, not what I think. In the name of Jesus, The Truth, Amen.*

## BOMBARDED BY A RELENTLESS PARADE

*Do not conform any longer to the pattern of this world, but be transformed by the renewing of your mind. Then you will be able to test and approve what God's will is—his good, pleasing, and perfect will.*
Romans 12:2, NIV

hat becomes commonplace changes me. I can remember the times when I hurt inside if anyone took God's name in vain, when I winced at some of the four-letter words so commonly used on TV today—words I never allowed to enter my home by any other way. I never tolerated a child's playmate or a crude adult friend using those words, but now I am frequently unaware of the vile language so casually used on the TV in my family room

And God's standard for marriage is steadily eroding as the ever-present marriage triangle on TV now involves not just the bad guy but our heroes, the "nice guys." Sleeping overnight with someone else's wife or husband doesn't carry a hint that it might be wrong. And little by little we are a bit less shocked as we grow accustomed to that kind of lifestyle.

In today's popular music there has crept in a gradual changing of moral values. We find ourselves actually sympathizing with the lovers who have to keep their "beautiful" love a secret till they both are free from the selfish culprits to whom they are married. And the young woman alone in her room at night convincingly laments that there is some man out there missing what she has to give.

I recall the startled expression on the face of a member of my Sunday School class when we read Jesus' words in Matthew 5:28 that "whosoever looketh on a woman to lust after her hath committed adultery with her already in his heart." Horrified, he exploded, "Does it really say that?" Yes, God's "flee fornication" still stands, no matter how much the world tries to change our thinking.

I wonder how many Christian young people are getting their moral standards from this relentless parade, and how many adults unwittingly lower their ideals because of this invasion by the world. And when does turning our heads and ignoring it change into condoning? Changed—first in our thinking and then in our actions.

*Dear God, please help me. I'm constantly bombarded by a relentless parade of ungodly people trying to invade my mind. Keep me always sensitive to Your standard of holiness—and resisting the world. In Jesus' name, Amen.*

## GULLIBLE—IF IT'S IN PRINT

*Timothy, guard what has been entrusted to your care.
Turn away from godless chatter and the opposing
ideas of what is falsely called knowledge, which some
have professed and in so doing have wandered from
the faith. Grace be with you.*
1 Timothy 6:20 21, NIV

 returned missionary shared with me that he felt God was calling him to translate good literature to send to the nationals he had just left. "They believe anything that is in print," he lamented. But it happens here in America, too. A national denominational women's executive said to me one day, "What can we do about the gullibility of our women? Now that women are 'thinking for themselves' they are reading and studying everything they can get their hands on. And they are believing anything, as long as it's in print, swallowing everything printed under the name of 'Christian.'"

We should test every book we read by the Bible's standards, but the tendency today is to make the Bible's teachings fit into those of a book—secular or religious. In a Sunday School class a teacher was using a popular secular book, attempting to conform biblical concepts to the ideas expressed in the book.

After a few sessions of this study, a woman became extremely agitated and said, "I personally studied this material in a seminar conducted by the author, and by 9 A.M. he was 'bombed.' And we Christians are evaluating the Bible by what this alcoholic's book says!" Many of us act as if the Bible is on trial, whereas we should judge every book by what the Bible says. And this includes Christian books. An internationally known Christian psychologist startled me one day when he said that he didn't know a single Christian book that did not have in it something he considered to be contrary to the Scripture.

We must evaluate *all* the teachings in a book. A national Christian radio personality told me last week that she had been reprimanded for reviewing a certain book on the air. In her hurried perusal of that book, she had missed the one anti-scriptural teaching in it. But she learned that it was necessary to check out all the teachings of any book before she reviewed it. I've heard people say in defense of an author, "But that book has so much good in it." Great. Take what is good and true, and accept it. But we must reject anything, even from our favorite author, that is not consistent with biblical truth. A lot of truth in a book doesn't automatically make everything in the book true.

*Dear God, I don't ever want to be gullible. I need great spiritual discernment from You, dear Lord. Don't let me be blinded by a fleshly or persuasive personality peddling what they think. In Jesus' name, Amen.*

## ADVICE FROM OTHER PEOPLE

*It is better to trust in the Lord
than to put confidence in man.*
Psalm 118:8, KJV

 went home and cried after receiving some advice from another person at a retreat. In a little exercise of giving something to each other she said to me, "I give you a spirit of adventure."

I was crushed. "Lord," I prayed, "have I missed it that much that people think I need a spirit of adventure?" Reviewing that very month, I realized how wrong that advice had been. I had turned fifty— which in itself took a lot of courage. And I enrolled in my first seminary class, started speaking on a then very misunderstood subject in churches and schools— "The Dangers of the Occult," organized my first St. Paul telephone prayer chain, conceived and planned the first of the annual Founder's Week luncheons for women at our college and seminary— and on the list went.

I'm sure I needed advice, but a spirit of adventure was not it. I could have used "Learn to say no," "One thing at a time," or, "Try eight hours of sleep some night."

Psalm 118:8 says, "It is better to trust in the Lord than to put confidence in man." Advice from other people can chisel away at us until we are reduced to a fraction of all that God intended for us to be. God's wisdom enlarges, matures, and fulfills us.

The worth of people's advice is determined by their source of wisdom. There is much Christian counsel that is worthwhile and beneficial. But if the counseling is contrary to the Bible's instructions or from the person's "I thinks," it can never change us into the persons God intends us to be. "And my speech and my preaching was not with enticing words of man's wisdom, but in demonstration of the Spirit and of power; that your faith should not stand in the wisdom of men, but in the power of God" (1 Cor. 2:4-5).

How precious is the counsel of the godly to us, and how good to be changed by it; but even Job (Job 38:1-2), Christ (Matt. 16:21-23), and Peter and John (Acts 4:18-20) had to firmly reject being changed by advice from people so that they could follow God's leading in their lives.

Changed? Yes! But by the only infallible, consistently reliable Source—the Lord.

*Dear Lord, You know how much I appreciate and listen to my advisors passing on to me what You are telling them. But please help me to be so in tune with You myself and Your Word's teaching that I will be able to recognize—and reject—what is not from You. In Jesus' name, Amen.*

# I'M UNIQUE

*So then every one of us shall give account of himself to God.*
Romans 14:12, KJV

ow I thank God that He created me a unique individual. Nobody else is just like me. And God's finished product, "Me," is different from any other He has planned.

But I must realize that every other Christian is unique, too, and God is changing them according to His divine blueprint. I have a tendency to feel that if some changing is right for me, then God must want everybody else to change in the same way. But that is not true. The way the Lord changes me does not automatically become a pattern for every other person. Only the omniscient God of heaven has clearly in mind the finished product for each of His children, and I must let Him, not Evelyn, be every individual's Source of wisdom. I must direct others to the Designer of their individual blueprint—the Lord of glory.

And having God's unique blueprint in my spiritual genes also makes me responsible; accountable for all the potential He put in me; answerable to God for how I let Him change me into what He ultimately wants me to be. "So then every one of us shall give account of himself to God" (Rom. 14:12).

This places the ultimate responsibility on each individual before God. In the final judgment each person will answer for himself. God has only children, no grandchildren. I will be accountable only for me— only for what I have allowed God to do in and through me. "Oh, Lord, change ME!"

*Dear Father in heaven, I keep wondering why You didn't create me more like Jesus in the first place—instead of expecting me to do all this changing. But I'm willing so I will be able to give an account of myself—not just redeemed, but not having missed what You had planned for me to become.*

# CHANGED— SO THAT . . .

*May the words of my mouth and the meditation*
*of my heart be pleasing in your sight,*
*O LORD, my Rock and my Redeemer.*
Psalm 19:14, NIV

 hange for the sake of change doesn't make much sense. In the natural realm, the new isn't always better than the old. Romans 12:2, however, gives us the reason for our being transformed by the renewing of our minds: *that ye may prove what is that good, and acceptable, and perfect, will of God"* (italics mine). This is that will of God which is in itself pleasing to Him and which results in actions on the part of His children that are pleasing and *acceptable* to Him. Changed so that all the words of my mouth and the meditations of my heart are acceptable in the sight of my Lord (Ps. 19:14). Changed, so that I will be and do what He wants.

Changed, also, that others may observe my behavior—which has been changed because my thinking is acceptable to God (1 Peter 3:1-2). So often our lives reflect "Do as I say, not as I do," but the book of 1 Peter says my husband (and other people) are changed and won when they see my changed life.

A psychiatrist who attended one of my prayer seminars wouldn't accept anything I said until she saw me in action with other people. Not knowing she could read lips, I questioned her intense gaze from the other side of the room as I interacted with and counseled several different people after a dinner party following the seminar. My speech at the seminar was of little value to her until she saw me prove myself in action. James says a person who is really wise shows it out of a good life (3:13).

*Dear Lord, Father, I have so far to go. I fall so short of what You want me to be. Please keep changing me on this earth until there won't be so much left to change when I see my Jesus. In His holy name, Amen.*

# Gaining through God's "So Thats"

*Oh, the depth of the riches both of the wisdom and
knowledge of God! How unsearchable are His
judgments and unfathomable His ways!*
Romans 11:33, NASB

o you always win? Or do you sometimes lose?
If you do, God is in the business of turning
your losses into gains.

It was many years ago, as I lay fretting in my hospital bed recovering from surgery, that God taught
me the gaining through losing principle. I was struggling against having to miss all the exciting things He
was doing in our church. As I reached for my radio, I
searched the local stations until I heard the familiar
voice of a pastor friend chatting to us "shut-ins."
Suddenly he said, "The title of this poem is 'Gaining
Through Losing.'"

And I was about to discover one of the greatest of
all discoveries about God—as he read:

*I asked God for strength, that I might achieve,*
  *I was made weak, that I might learn humbly to obey,*
*I asked for health, that I might do greater things,*
  *I was given infirmity, that I might do better things.*

*I asked for riches, that I might be happy,*
  *I was given poverty, that I might be wise.*
*I asked for power, that I might have the praise of men,*
  *I was given weakness, that I might feel the need of God.*
*I asked for all things, that I might enjoy life,*
  *I was given life, that I might enjoy all things.*
*I got nothing that I asked for—but everything I had hoped for.*

  *Almost despite myself, my unspoken prayers were answered.*

*I am, among all men, most richly blessed.*


Suddenly I came alive. I had discovered God's "so that" principle!

I have discovered in the Bible that every facet in God's dealing with His people seems to include a "so that." In effect God says to us, "I am permitting this unpleasant experience *so that* you may gain a new insight, *so that* you will be *richer* in your experiences and thereby help someone going through a similar problem." Nothing with God is haphazard, coincidental, or happenstance. Problems in our lives do not mean that God has lost control or that He is no longer on His throne, but they give us the glorious opportunity to prove God's "so thats"—so that we might gain through our losses.

*Dear Father, I bow in awe before You, realizing that every hard thing in my life has had Your "so that." Thank You for my losses that produced Your better things in and for me. In Jesus' name, Amen.*

## My "So Thats" for Others

*Now I want you to know, brethren,*
*that my circumstances have turned out*
*for the greater progress of the gospel.*
Philippians 1:12, NASB

rom the time I first read the "Gaining through Losing" poem (found in the last reading) to now, I have been discovering God's "so thats." Through the years God has unfolded some of the magnitude of this principle to me. When we let Him, He takes our losses and shows us His great "so thats"—so that we can have or be more than before. He works our losses all out for our gains. That day, I thought the poem applied to the giving of my body to the Lord, but that was only the immediate result. Today, I could fill a whole book with God's "so thats"—how He takes our losses and turns them into gains.

What do those two little words *so that* really mean? *The Random House Dictionary of the English Language* (p. 1350) gives these definitions for *so that*: "in order that", "with the effect or result." It involves the reasons, the whys of life. Even the little word *that* is defined as "expressing cause or reason, purpose or aim, result or consequence" (p. 1470).

The Bible is full of God's "so thats." Paul tells us that the things which happened to him had "fallen out rather unto the furtherance of the gospel; *so that* my bonds in Christ are manifest in all the palace and in all other places" (Phil. 1:12-13). Jesus, before restoring sight to the man blind from birth, must have startled His disciples with His answer to their question, "Who did sin, this man, or his parents?" He replied, "Neither has this man sinned, nor his parents; but *that* the works of God should be made manifest in him" (John 9:3).

Jesus summed up the "so that" principle with His words, "Whosoever will lose his life for My sake shall find it" (Matt. 16:26.) Yes, Jesus said you must lose your life *so that* you can find it. It will be *through* your loss that you can actually gain—so that you can help others gain too.

*Dear Lord, You have shown me so many times that the final "so that" reason for my hard things is not for me but for others. Thanks for the privilege of teaching and helping others find Your "so thats" for them— like You taught me. In Jesus' name, Amen.*

## Jesus' "So That" Principle

*Then Jesus said to his disciples, "If anyone would
come after me, he must deny himself
and take up his cross and follow me."*
Matthew 16:24, NIV

esus said that if anybody will come after Me,
triumph with Me, and experience the victory I
am going to experience, there is a formula to follow:
First, *deny yourself.* But what is myself? Is it my
personal ambitions, my self-seekings, my self-
assertions—doing what I like to do? Must I volun-
tarily abandon all these? Must I always say "no" to
me?

After I had struggled in prayer one morning, I sat
alone reading through John's account of Christ's resurrection and the events which followed. I stopped
abruptly when I came to "Peter . . . lovest thou me
more than these?" (John 21:15) Peter, with the other
disciples, had gone back to his former occupation—
fishing. When he recognized Jesus on the shore
preparing breakfast, Peter, having denied not himself
but Jesus on the way to the cross, jumped into the
water in his eagerness to reach Christ. When breakfast was finished, Jesus turned to Peter and asked

that piercing question, "Lovest thou Me more than these?"

I pondered the "more than these" for a long time. I wondered what *my* "more than these" might be. *My* dreams, *my* house, *my* loved ones?

I thought of my children whom I love so deeply. My heart was aching as I silently prayed, "How could I stop loving *them,* Lord? Lose them for Your sake? My own flesh and blood?" Then suddenly, He clearly said, "*More*—don't love them *more* than you love Me." And then I knew that for me, "these things" were anything I put ahead of Him—my priorities.

When we give the most important thing in our lives (material possessions, a human relationship, or a circumstance) to God for His will, many fear that God will automatically take away all they give Him. But that is not usually the case. God only wants us to be willing to give up all for Him, to love Him more than we love all these other things.

I have found that when I really learn to do this, the process of gaining through losing starts in my life. Then, and only then, do I begin to find *life* as Jesus intended it to be for me.

*Dear holy God, You know how dearly I love my family. But I do love You more—much, much more! Please always keep my priorities straight while You still are giving me the awesome love for my family—and You! In Jesus' name, Amen.*

# Take Up Your Cross

*I am crucified with Christ:*
*nevertheless I live; yet not I, but Christ liveth in me.*
Galatians 2:20, KJV

 fter denying yourself, the second part of Jesus' formula for finding life is not getting rid of something, but taking up something—your cross. The disciples knew well what taking up a cross meant. Many times they had seen the condemned carry the instruments on which they would be killed. Did Jesus mean that we were to take up the life for which the cross stood—a life of sacrifice? Did He mean that even when our cross would be bearing a trial that points to even a worse one to come? Are we still to pick it up willingly?

While at a retreat, God explained to me a little of His secret of gaining life through the losing process of the cross. In the wee hours of the night, I was praying about living the victorious Christian life. Suddenly, the chiming of bells filled the still night air with "Jesus, lover of my soul, let me to Thy bosom fly." I arose and stood on the porch in silence, spellbound as the full moon glistened. My eyes looked heavenward, pleading with God. "I can't live this life," I prayed, "I can't do it."

"No," came the answer, "but Christ can live it in you." Then, as I waited for more, God brought Galatians 2:20 to my mind. The mystery of that verse began to unravel before me.

I am crucified with Christ. Nevertheless I *live*. Yet not I, but *Christ lives in me.*

Not just into a cross experience, but Jesus living His life in me—resurrected, victorious life!

The losses of life don't need to stop at being losses. In God's hands they can be *so that* we can gain life— real life—not only for eternity, but also for right here, today.

*Losing* my self-seeking *so that* I can *gain* Christ's fulfilling, joyous, abundant life? That's quite a bargain!

*Dear Lord Jesus, it is absolutely incredible to have You living in me—victorious, resurrected Lord! Keep teaching me every way I can lose my life for Your sake, so that I can have more and more of Your abundant life. In Your name, dear Jesus, Amen.*

## POWER OF CHRIST

*My grace is sufficient for you,*
*for my power is made perfect in weakness."*
2 Corinthians 12:9a, NIV

was scheduled to bring a prayer seminar to Agape Atlanta, the pilot project of the International "Here's Life" undertaking. Six hundred Christians were to gather the next day to learn the power of prayer for this endeavor. Since it was one of my early attempts to teach all the precepts of my book, *What Happens When Women Pray,* in one day, I had planned carefully. I had timed and recorded the points which could be included on each subject, sifted to find material which best illustrated these points, and then separated each subject into individual file folders to keep the five-to-six hours of lecturing and prayer exercises organized.

Just before going to sleep on the night before the seminar, I was reading 2 Corinthians 12. When I came to the end of verse 9, "my power is made perfect in weakness," I closed my Bible, held it close, and prayed a simple prayer: "Lord, tomorrow I want the power of Christ, only the power of Christ." Then I went to sleep with that prayer on my lips and on my heart.

The next morning I awoke aghast. My eyes were swelling! I knew that if the swelling continued, I would not be able to read any of my so carefully prepared notes! Envisioning the potential confusion, I panicked and started praying desperately that God would take care of the problem. Then He gently asked me a question: "What did you pray last night?"

"Oh," I said almost aloud as I remembered—"I want the power of Christ tomorrow." Then a new kind of prayer emerged: "Lord, if You are going to show me the power of Christ by my inability to refer to my notes all day, OK. I'm willing to speak to 600 people and trust You to tell me what to say." The swelling stopped at the point of my barely being able to see. I relaxed, and went to that seminar without the ability to glance at my notes—but with a tremendous sense of the power of Christ resting in me.

*Dear Lord, thanks that every time I need Your strength to serve You, You never have or ever will fail me. I pray you would use my weakness to demonstrate Your power. In Jesus' powerful name, Amen.*

# LESSONS FROM GOD'S "NO" ANSWER

*I will boast all the more gladly about my weaknesses,*
*so that Christ's power may rest on me.*
2 Corinthians 12:9b, NIV

n 2 Corinthians, Paul explained that the Lord told him how a "no" answer would be turned into gain. God was teaching Paul two of life's greatest lessons.

The first lesson Jesus taught Paul was, *"My grace is sufficient for you"* (see 2 Cor. 12:9). As long as he had this infirmity (evidently up to the time of his death), there would be grace enough to cover all the difficulties brought on by it. How Paul would need that lesson, not only in his infirmity, but also in the trials, imprisonments, shipwrecks, and eventual martyrdom that were to come!

Then in His answer, the Lord taught Paul a second powerful lesson. *"My strength is made perfect in weakness"* (v. 9). (Paul repeated this thought in verse 10 by concluding with, "for when I am weak, then am I strong.") It is not physical strength that counts, but the power of Christ which pitches its tent over our bodies when we are weak. What was Paul's (or my) maximum strength compared with Christ's omnipotence? In comparison to Christ's infinite, limitless power, all the strength we could ever muster, rolled into one gigantic push, would pale like a firefly competing with a nuclear explosion. What did Paul gain when the Lord said "no" to his being at his best physically? What do I gain? *The strength of the omnipotent Christ!*

Listening to my husband preach over the years, I have become acutely aware of the unusual, powerful strength of his messages when his body has not been at its best. Somehow when there has been no way Chris could deliver a sermon in his own strength, that was the time the Lord stepped in and poured out His power through Christ.

If you are losing what you think is best for you by getting an apparent "no" answer from the Lord, take heart. It was because Paul's thorn in the flesh remained that the Lord could show him His mysterious dealings with His own—how He equips us through our seeming-losses. How much more powerful, effective, and fruitful Paul was because of that "no" answer! Enough grace and enough power!

*Dear Lord, compared to Your omnipotence, I am unbelievably weak. Give me the wisdom to understand how Your "no" answers give me the privilege of experiencing the power of Christ actually on and in me. In Jesus' name, Amen.*

# Removed Hindrances

*Therefore I take pleasure in infirmities, in reproaches,*
*in necessities, in persecutions, in distresses for Christ's*
*sake: for when I am weak, then am I strong.*
2 Corinthians 12:10, KJV

'm fascinated by street sweepers—those massive lumbering machines which loosen and vacuum up debris on the roads. Knowing the magnitude of the task to which the Lord called Paul on the Damascus Road, doesn't it seem logical that He would have sent His supernatural "street cleaner" to dislodge and remove all the hindrances in Paul's pathway? He could have swept the path clean before sending Paul onto it, or at least vacuumed the obstacles as they confronted Paul. But the New Testament tells us that God did neither. We see rather that they were left there—deliberately.

The whole list which Paul adds to the "infirmities" was left in his path intentionally *so that* he could learn and grow from them. Left *so that* the power would be Christ's omnipotence and not Paul's puny human strength. From man's point of view they were losses, but in God's hands they were turned into gigantic *gains.*

I guess the "narrow way" on which Jesus sends me on my journey to heaven hasn't been swept clean either. Even when the source of annoyance is Satan, as was Job's before the cross and Paul's after the cross, God can and does use that *loss* for *gain* in me too.

Which one of us at some time in life has not wished for, even longed for, a life like Paul's? Full of adventure, fruit, rewards! Changing the world in which he lived! Then influencing people all over Planet Earth! Could the secret be that Paul learned and accepted God's *gaining through losing* principle? God's *so thats?*

What did Paul lose? Being delivered from infirmities, reproaches, necessities, persecutions, distresses. What did he *gain?* Christ's grace and power and strength—resting on Him!

Have you discovered God's divine "so that" in your life?

*Dear God, thank You that You don't remove all the obstacles in my life when I ask You to. Keep me willing to accept the bumps and hindrances so that I can gain Christ's awesome grace and power.*
*In His name, Amen.*

# "Who" Not "Why"

*"My ears had heard of you,*
*but now my eyes have seen you."*
Job 42:5, NIV

ave you ever asked "why" during your trials? Job's "why" questions were never completely answered, and the mystery of the drama of heaven between God and Satan was never revealed to him.

But whatever the reason for God's allowing the grief really doesn't matter—for it was in Job's sorrow that God chose to reveal Himself in new and magnanimous ways. As I settled down to read the way God revealed Himself to Job in the 38th and 39th chapters, God kept getting bigger and bigger and bigger. How Job must have felt himself shrinking and shrinking as his knowledge of God kept expanding and expanding.

When God finished giving Job the new revelation of who He really was, Job could cry, "My ears had heard of you, but now my eyes have seen you" (Job 42:5, NIV). Then Job suddenly knew all was well with him and the whole universe! God was, and always has been, in control. The combatant turned into the worshiper. And all of Job's "whys" turned to "Who."

During the first years of my marriage, I found myself almost drowning in a sea of "why" questions as trials flooded over me. But gradually I detected an emerging pattern. It was in those times of engulfment in a sea of sorrows that God would speak to me in a new way. Little by little I saw it. God was choosing to reveal Himself to me at those times, in each instance showing me a deeper, more profound side of Himself—one I'd never seen before.

It has been many, many years since I have asked God "why" in my trials. With a shocking report from a doctor, a calamity in a child's life, or some shattering news in the family, I find myself searching for that "more of my God." I, with Job, have *heard* much of God, but it has always been in those difficult times of my life that I have *seen* Him—ready and eager to reveal more of Himself to me. What a fabulous gain through my *losses!*

Have your "whys" turned to "Who"?

*Dear Lord, please forgive me whenever I slip back into self-pity, asking You* why. *What a deep privilege it has been to have You show me a more profound and wonderful side of Yourself when I stopped asking* why. *Thank You, dear Lord. In Jesus' name, Amen.*

# God of the Grapes

*"I am the true vine, and My Father is the vinedresser.*
*Every branch in Me that does not bear fruit, He takes*
*away; and every branch that bears fruit He prunes it,*
*that it may bear more fruit."*

John 15:1-2, NASB

s we rode to a seminar in California, my hostess and I passed field after field of ugly stumps with wires strung above them. Finally I asked her, "What on earth are those?"

"Oh," she said with obvious pride, "they're our grapevines!"

As I gazed on them in silence, my heart cried out, "Father, am I that ugly when you are pruning me?"

Jesus' words from John 15 kept whirling around in my mind. "I am the true vine, and My Father is the vinedresser. . . . Every branch that bears fruit, He prunes it . . ." (John 15:1-2). It is the Father, said Jesus, who holds the pruning knife in His hand and prunes those who are His own.

As Jesus' words kept marching through my mind, a surprising thought emerged: it is those of us who are already bearing fruit whom God prunes! So why the pruning process? So *that* we can bear *more* fruit!

It was winter when I saw those ugly stumps.

Suddenly God showed me there are winters in my life too. As with grapes, all the seasons are represented in our lives also. There are dormant periods when the "sap" has retreated, and sadly not much is happening through me. Then there is the growing season, that time when I'm being nourished by the Vine while the fruit is ripening and I spoil it by impatiently plucking it. I mostly don't care for the pruning season when God's sharp knife mercilessly prunes away the abundant leaves and long stems of my past time of productivity. No, I definitely prefer the glorious, rewarding fruit-bearing season.

Then I wondered about God. Does His heart bleed when He knows the only way to produce more fruit is to get out His pruning knife? Does it hurt Him more than it hurts me? Does He like the fruit-bearing season best too?

Mentally I dug into my past losses—sorrow, suffering, lost babies, surgery, family difficulties—and wondered if some, or many of them, had occurred because God had put His pruning tools to work. I had definitely been left feeling like a bare, bleeding stump after those experiences. Yes, I had been pruned by the hand of the divine Vinedresser!

*Dear Lord, You are the One who does the pruning in my life—so that I will bear more fruit for You. Lord, I trust You completely because You alone know why it is not fruit-bearing season in my life—what I want all the time. In Jesus' name, Amen.*

# TOUCHED BY GOD

*"The hand of God hath touched me."*
Job 19:21, KJV

 have been touched by the hand of God in so many different ways. I've felt His strong, supporting hand beneath me when I've crumpled in grief, and have been securely held in the hollow of His hand when life engulfed me. When there was no power of my own, I've felt the omnipotence of His hand. I've known His firm hand steering the course of my life, experienced the restraining of His hand when I would run ahead. I've felt the tenderness of the divine Gardener's hand pressing mine, and been made well by the touch of the hand of the Great Physician. And I've felt His cooling hand on my hot, feverish brow. But I have also felt the sting of the pruning knife in the omniscient Vinedresser's hand.

Somehow in our imaginations we have invented a god whose hand gives only love pats. But this is not what the Bible tells us. Job, at the low ebb in his suffering, cried, "The hand of God hath touched me" (Job 19:21). Paul, after being touched by God on the Damascus Road, was blinded for a season. Jacob, before he crossed the Jabbok River to be reunited with his estranged brother, Esau, wrestled and felt the touch of God on his thigh, and he was permanently crippled—by God. As the sinew shrank, Jacob said, "I have seen God face to face" (Gen. 32:30).

While touring the Holy Land I felt God's presence the most at the Jabbok River where Jacob had wrestled all night. I slipped away down the bank and sat alone, motionless, absorbing every bit of that Presence. The surrounding hills formed a natural amphitheater; and reverberating, echoing across the valley from hill to hill—God!

I pondered in that place: *Was losing the full use of a part of his physical body and limping for the rest of his life worth what Jacob gained?* The answer was overwhelmingly "yes." Personally blessed by God! Blessed beyond his fondest dreams. Then given a new name. Not Supplanter now, but Israel. "A nation and a company of nations shall be of thee, and kings shall come out of thy loins" (35:11). And he was given power with God—and power with men.

*Dear Father, I enjoy Your love pats so much. But when Your touch hurts me, I too come face to face with Your incredible, holy presence—in humble adoration and gratitude. In Jesus' name, Amen.*

# THE EXPERT PRUNER

*"I am the true vine, and my Father is the gardener."*
John 15:1, NIV

ecently my friend Jane brought me a small purple passion plant which she had started from her own. While I was anxiously waiting for it to grow in its new environment, it suddenly shot straight up, resembling a purple and green bean pole. Common sense told me to pinch off the top, but I could not muster the courage.

For several weeks I approached it, fingers poised, only to lose my nerve and retreat. I could not bear to hurt my little plant. Finally I steeled myself, gritted my teeth, and pinched. To my surprise, in just one week many new shoots appeared on the stalk, filling out the ugly leafless spots. But later when I returned from a speaking tour, to my horror, a long sprout had shot out from the top at a very awkward angle, and the main stem had compensated by bending in the opposite direction to keep from falling over. Again I resolutely gathered all my courage—and pinched. Then I came to one conclusion—I am not an expert pruner. I just don't know how to do it.

It takes an expert to prune effectively. The wife of a grape grower said to me, "Do you want to know something about pruning? Very few people can prune. We go to great trouble to hire the very best expert available."

God is the Expert Pruner. The supernatural divine Professional. He never pinches or cuts too soon lest He damage my tender branch. He never lets me get too far out of control before He draws His knife. He knows just how far to let me sprawl. He understands which part of me and just exactly how much of that part He must prune. How precious to know that the care of me as Jesus' branch will never have to be entrusted to a human vinedresser. My Vinedresser is an Expert. He is God.

*Dear Father, how good it is not to have to struggle to find a human who can prune me correctly. Thanks for caring enough for Your child to always give me Your expert, divine, perfect pruning—not too much, not too little, not too soon, not too late. In Jesus' name, Amen.*

# The Sovereign Pruner

*I know, O LORD, that Thy judgments are righteous,*
*And that in faithfulness Thou hast afflicted me.*
Psalm 119:75, NASB

ince pruning means "purging by removal," "cleansing by separation from," and "cutting away living parts," we must ask, does God just *allow* or does He actually *do something* that hurts His own? Here is one of the theological battles of the ages.

The Bible states that God was able to save His Son, Jesus, from the death of the cross (Heb. 5:7). Jesus even cried to His Father *who was able to save Him.* But God did not. It was the Father's will that His Son should suffer and die. (We know that it was Satan who caused Christ's death by bringing sin into the world and making redemption on the cross necessary.) But God could have chosen a less severe method of redemption. God could also have prevented Job's suffering by saying "no" to Satan. But He did not. So did He cause Job's grief?

To be sure, I sometimes bring suffering upon myself. When I break God's moral or physical laws carelessly or deliberately, I reap the consequences. Sometimes sorrow is the result of a natural course of events here on this fallen planet. But sometimes it is of God. The Old Testament abounds with instances of God sending affliction (see Num. 14:28, 33; Pss. 66:10-11; 119:71, 75; Isa. 9:1).

At a convention this past summer, I asked Joni Eareckson Tada if she would give me a quote on this subject. She cheerily responded, "Sure. Come to my room when I'm through speaking tonight." Still in braces from her shoulders to her hands and feet, she lay on her bed talking to me about questioning God and praying to be healed from the paralysis which resulted from her diving accident. Then she recounted her climb up through those reactions to her present beautiful relationship with God. As we discussed whether God just allowed these things or actually had a part in sending them, she suddenly broke forth in a beaming smile and exclaimed, "Oh, that isn't even a good question, is it? *He's sovereign!* He's in control of everything!"

Sovereign! The expert, supernatural Vinedresser who gives the perfect season, the perfect nourishment, the perfect protection, and the perfect pruning—to His precious branches.

*Dear Lord, thank You for being sovereign God. Thank You that, although You are able to prevent everything bad from happening to me, sometimes You deliberately send or allow them—so that You can accomplish Your better things. In Jesus' name, Amen.*

# Fruit Bearing

*Brothers, as an example of patience in the face of
suffering, take the prophets who spoke in the name of
the Lord. As you know, we consider blessed those who
have persevered. You have heard of Job's perseverance
and have seen what the Lord finally brought about.
The Lord is full of compassion and mercy.*
James 5:10-11, NIV

 fter learning about God's "pruning," are you
saying you don't want any part of a God like
that? Are you thinking, *With a friend like that, who
needs enemies?* James explained in his epistle that
when we can look back and see what the Lord has
brought about through suffering, we will realize that
He really was good all along.

Jesus explained that God's reason for pruning is
never to hurt us but to produce more fruit. That glorious season we love so much. Fruit-bearing!
Accomplished by God's all-loving, all-wise process!

What is fruit in our lives? In the New Testament,
fruit occasionally means the winning of souls. But
usually it means what is produced in our personality—*our potential.* Those visibly expressed character
traits which the Holy Spirit produces in us—"love,
joy, peace, long-suffering, gentleness, goodness,
faith, meekness, self control" (Gal. 5:22-23).

It is amazing to study Scripture and see *how* these personality gains are produced. James wrote, "My brethren, count it all joy when you fall into various trials, knowing this, that the testing of your faith worketh patience. But let patience have her perfect work that you may be perfect and entire, lacking nothing" (James 1:2-4). Our potential is fulfilled through trials. Paul wrote, "But we glory in tribulations also; knowing that tribulation worketh patience; and patience, experience; and experience, hope" (Rom. 5:3-4). Penned beside Romans 8:28 ("All things work together for good. . . ") in my old Bible is the simple, now fading word, "Judy," the child we lost in infancy, with an arrow pointing to the pruning verse John 15:2. Pruned! For my good. To produce fruit—more Christlikeness—in me.

In California I was told that if grapes are not pruned, a fuzzy, ugly, hairlike growth appears on the branches of the vine. I may think everything being produced in my life is the luscious fruit of the Spirit. But God, seeing the real me, gets out His pruning knife and cuts away at the branches.

It is through the pruning that we *gain the rare privilege of actually realizing our full potential!*

*Dear Father in heaven, thank You for allowing me to see Your working all things together for my good since losing that baby so many years ago now. Truly You knew my potential, and are producing fruit of the Spirit in me through it all. In Jesus' precious name, Amen.*

## SPIRITUAL FRUIT OF THE WOMB

*Lift up your eyes, and look on the fields; for they are*
*white already to harvest, and he that reapeth . . .*
*gathereth fruit unto life eternal.*
John 4:35-36, KJV

n addition to fruits of the Spirit, there are some examples in the Bible of the other kind of fruit being produced in our lives. There is the fruit of the womb—spiritual offspring. This comes as a result of being a witness. Jesus told His disciples, "Lift up your eyes, and look on the fields; for they are white already to harvest, and he that reapeth . . . gathereth *fruit* unto life eternal" (John 4:35-36, italics added). With this same idea, Paul expressed his desire to visit the Romans that he might have some *fruit* among them (see Rom. 1:13).

It was because of Mary and Martha's grief that Jesus had the opportunity to demonstrate His power at the grave of Lazarus which produced the fruit of souls. "Many of the Jews who came to Mary [and Martha], and had seen the things which Jesus did, believed on Him" (John 11:45; see also 12:11).

At an annual convention of the auxiliary of the World Home Bible League in one of Chicago's large motels, the previous manager had overbooked. As a result 2,000 women waited for hours for rooms, some being shuttled to less desirable hotels and arriving back late for meetings. Torrential rain had flooded the below-ground-level convention room. Just two hours before the first session began, maintenance people had siphoned two inches of water from the floor. The 94-degree temperature and an inadequate air-conditioning system for a crowd that size had turned the room into a literal steam bath. Disaster reigned.

Just before I closed the last session, the new manager asked for time on our program. After explaining that his predecessor had lost his job because of the frightful overbooking, he thanked those ladies profusely for their beautiful spirit all that weekend. "If I had had this many traveling salesmen, they would have been fistfighting in the halls over the rooms. But not one of you complained once." Then—to thunderous applause—he said, "In fact, ladies, you have made a believer out of me!"

*Gained*—the privilege of being one of the branches God chooses to prune—*so that* I can realize my full potential of what I can be—*so that* I can bear eternal fruit!

*Dear God, keep me constantly aware that people will want to accept Jesus only if they see Him living in me. Make me what I need to be so that there will be much precious fruit of souls for eternity. In the name of our Savior, Jesus, Amen.*

# GOD IS GOOD?

*Though he brings grief, he will show compassion, so great is his unfailing love. For he does not willingly bring affliction or grief to the children of men.*
Lamentations 3:32-33, NIV

ack in 1943 my mother-in-law, 42 years old with two young children and a grown son away at war, answered the phone early one morning. It was the family doctor bearing the message that her husband, recovering from minor surgery, had just been found dead in his hospital bed. Being in the room with her, I listened in awe to her spontaneous response to that shocked doctor: "I still say God is good."

Yes, God is good. "Though he brings grief, he will show compassion, so great is his unfailing love. For he does not willingly bring affliction or grief to the children of men" (Lam. 3:32-33, NIV). But *His pruning is always to develop our full potential!*

Looking back at God's dual role of allowing and causing in my life, can I still say I love Him? Yes, with Job I can truthfully say, "Though He slay me, yet will I trust in Him" (Job 13:15). But at 4 o'clock the other morning, a thought occurred to me. *After all the pruning seasons in my life where God seemingly left me a bleeding, ugly stump, do I still like Him?*

There is quite a difference between my loving God and liking what He does. But even after all these years that God has allowed testing and has actually pruned me (admittedly to bear fruit), do I still *like* Him?

I wiggled down under the blankets, a smile crept over my face, and I exclaimed, "Hey, God I really *do* like You!"

In the light of your understanding God's roles of both allowing and doing the testing in your life, do *you* still like Him?

*Dear Father in heaven, looking back at the wonderful things You have done with my life because You never spared the pruning, I not only like You—*
*but I love You more than I ever thought possible.*
*In Jesus' precious name, Amen.*

# ALONENESS

*"Lo, I am with you alway, even unto the end of the world."*
Matthew 28:20, KJV

 loneness—the result of one of the greatest losses we can experience—that sometimes sudden and ever-deepening realization that we have been deprived of human companionship. The loss may come through death, separation, divorce, rebellion, or distance.

Aloneness is serious, frequently producing mild to severe physical, emotional, or mental stress. Numerous studies cite a definite correlation between loneliness and frequency of illness, length of hospitalization, admission to mental institutions, and a higher death rate. Writing on this subject, Dr. James J. Lynch, psychologist at the University of Maryland School of Medicine in Baltimore, states:

*Individuals who live alone—widows and widowers, divorced and single people—may be particularly vulnerable to stress and anxiety because they continuously lack the tranquilizing effect of human companionship* (The Broken Heart: The Medical Consequences of Loneliness, Basic Books).

Since the loss of human companionship at some time in life is inescapable, must the inevitable result always be complete loss for us? Must we endure these shattering losses alone? Is there no one to take up the role of companionship, to produce a tranquillity in us?

Yes, there is. Jesus. He is the One who promised those who love Him, "Lo, I am with you alway, even unto the end of the world" (Matt. 28:20). Always and forever! Companionship with Him is always available to us. He will never forsake His own, never rupture the relationship, never sever the bonds of love.

*Dear Lord Jesus, thank You for keeping Your promise to me that You would never forsake Your own. I know that all human relationships will be severed sooner or later, but You always will be there—even taking our hand when we step from human relationships to eternity with You! In Your faithfulness, Amen.*

## GOD: IN PROPORTION TO OUR NEEDS

*Praise be to the God and Father of our Lord Jesus
Christ, the Father of compassion and the God of all
comfort, who comforts us in all our troubles. . . .*
2 Corinthians 1:3-4, NIV

hen we *lose* the security and help of human
companionship, the *gain* we experience is that
fantastic proportion in which God gives of Himself to
us. It was in a hospital that I first learned this concept. Hospitalization produces a particular kind of
aloneness—the loss of the security of all familiar
human companionship. Absent too are all the familiar sounds, smells, and sights of our usual surround-
ings.

The night before surgery brings a very special kind
of aloneness. I was just 34 when I entered a hospital
for my first surgery. A lump in each breast foreshad-
owed an almost certain verdict of cancer. I had an
overwhelming need—and God knew it.

After my husband and all the hospital personnel
had left me, an amazing thing happened. It was not
just that I was opening myself up to Him more, but I
could suddenly sense God actually filling that stark,
white room with Himself. As I lay on that bed, I was

acutely aware of His presence permeating the room right up to the corners of the ceiling. He was there—all that I needed of Him. More of Him than I could ever remember experiencing before. *God understood the magnitude of my need, and came accordingly.*

When the chaplain came for his usual cheer-up-tomorrow's-surgery-rites, I didn't need him. Perhaps he didn't appreciate God usurping his rights, but God had already come!

What a *gain* in that *losing* situation! *Gained*—that unique privilege of having my room filled with the overwhelming presence of the God of the universe! The God even the heaven of the heavens cannot contain! And *gained*—the lifelong realization that no matter how great my need, God will infuse it to the extent that it needs filling. God coming in proportion to my need! Although the next day's surgery proved the tumors to be benign, I had learned one of life's most important lessons.

As I reflect on the gentle progression of God teaching me through hospital experiences, I realize that this principle had been in operation without my recognizing it all of my Christian life—God coming in proportion to my need.

*Dear Father in heaven, what an awesome privilege of having You, the God on Your throne in heaven, sensing my every need and actually coming to me in proportion to that need. I bow humbly before You, my God—with overwhelming awe. In Jesus' name, Amen.*

# DEATH:
## WHEN GOD SEVERS A HUMAN RELATIONSHIP

*The Lord is nigh unto them that are of a broken heart.*
Psalm 34:18, KJV

he greatest aloneness we ever experience is in the violent rending of loved ones by death. The loss is gargantuan. Almost unimaginable. *Can God* come in *that* great a proportion? *Does* He?

My first years of marriage seemed to be full of losses. Death was everywhere. Losing at three months the baby conceived on our honeymoon produced a psychological and, surprisingly, physical void entailing an adjustment that for me was deeper than any postpartum blues I later experienced—a body shocked at premature loss. Aloneness!

The loss of our second baby occurred at a period of great loss for the whole world—World War II, a time when we parted with people and things most dear to us—husbands, sons, doctors, sugar, tires, gasoline, shoes. For me it was a time of losing my husband to fight in a war just weeks after becoming pregnant.

This time the child was stillborn—a daughter. We had counted so heavily on that baby to fill the void, the aloneness, left when Chris' dad died so unexpectedly in his sleep following minor surgery just five weeks before. The new little grave dug next to his still fresh one turned Chris' second emergency leave into blackness and despair.

How God came in proportion to my need was amazing! Looking back, I realize there had been a deep, underlying assurance during those losses. Although at that young age I wasn't given to analyzing feelings and experiences, I remember the awful blackness being filled with an unusual presence. I recall vividly a special something, a quality in those bitter days of death that had not been there before. Nor after! It was just for that time. It was then that I had underlined Psalm 34:18 in my Bible: "The Lord is nigh unto them that are of a broken heart." I know now it was not a quality but a Person—God coming in proportion to my need.

*O dear God, there are no words to express the deep gratitude I feel in my heart for You actually coming to me in my blackest hours. Broken hearts are inevitable, but You will be there! In Jesus' precious name, Amen.*

## DEATH:
## WHEN GOD FILLS MY ALONENESS

*I thank Christ Jesus our Lord, who has given me*
*strength, that he considered me faithful,*
*appointing me to his service.*
1 Timothy 1:12, NIV

 hen God, in His infinite wisdom, knew that I had other needs in addition to being comforted with this enlarged proportion of Himself, He came in other, sometimes surprising, and almost shocking ways during my aloneness through death. The number of different methods God used to produce gain for me is fascinating to explore.

With my first pregnancy loss, that miscarriage, God filled my aloneness in a way I certainly had not expected. How startled I was when our very wise pastor visited me, assured me of his understanding, and then promptly asked me to be the superintendent of our upcoming Daily Vacation Bible School. I blinked in disbelief. How could he even think of anything else when I had just lost part of my very life? (Six pregnancies later, I smiled at how I had just known there would never be another baby.)

But life really hadn't come to an end. God showed me another way He comes and fills voids—*by calling me to serve others.* While I poured my whole being into those 300 eager pupils for two exhausting weeks, I almost completely forgot my own loss. And I certainly was no longer alone. Yes, God had come in proportion to my need, when I didn't even know what my need was—filling the void by calling me to serve others.

*Dear Father, how good of You to provide the healing of serving others when I felt life was so empty and hopeless. It certainly isn't the way I would have thought up. Thanks for being the all-wise God! In Jesus' name, Amen.*

## DEATH:
## WHEN GOD CALLS ME TO COUNSEL OTHERS

*For this reason, since the day we heard about you,*
*we have not stopped praying for you and asking God*
*to fill you with the knowledge of his will through all*
*spiritual wisdom and understanding.*

Colossians 1:9, NIV

ow God came in proportion to my need and produced a most important *gain* because of the *loss* of my stillborn baby wasn't to be realized till years later. He knew my future need, and was preparing me for my role of listening to the heart cries of many young wives as a seminar leader.

In one of my prayer seminars, a young wife of a seminary student stubbornly refused to pray for God's will in her life. In her bitter anger toward God, she belligerently explained to me, "We prayed and prayed for a baby, and finally God answered and I became pregnant. He even gave us a name for our baby. Then three months later, right at Christmas, I lost it. I will never pray 'God's will' in my life again."

After much listening and comforting, I finally said, "Did you ever stop to think that the purpose of that baby's life was perfectly fulfilled? God's purpose—to bring you as a future pastor's wife to a place of complete and total surrender to His will—the absolutely essential ingredient for an effective ministry."

Wide-eyed, she pondered . . . understood . . . and literally crumpled before God. Then she prayed, "Only *Your* will in my whole life. Take all of me—for Your holy will." What a privilege I had *gained* because of my similar and equally shattering losses!

*Dear Father, nothing is more empty and frequently offensive than advice from somebody who NEVER has walked in my shoes. Thank You for all the difficult things in my life that help me care for others—because I know how their pain feels. In Jesus' name, Amen.*

## God Explaining Why

*All things God works for the good of those who love him, who have been called according to his purpose.*
Romans 8:28, NIV

ll the ways God has come in proportion to my need have not only been for the future. During my third pregnancy-loss, God actually explained to me *right then* what my gain was through losing those three babies. At that time I had stayed in bed for 14 days with my feet elevated more than a foot, trying desperately not to lose a baby again. But I did.

That wasn't to be the last death-loss for us, but it marked the time I began to see *how* God fills the void with Himself. God was starting to show me the gains He had planned for me. Things finally began to come into focus, a focus that was to continue throughout my life.

It was in my utter hopelessness that I cried out to God for His "why." And He answered—coming in a gigantic way in proportion to my gigantic need. He flashed before me "Romans 8:28," who He was—the God who was working out all those losses for my good. To those who love Him—to those who are called according to His purpose. (See *What Happens When Women Pray,* chapter 6, for the complete story.) His *purpose.* But my *good?* Yes, it was God showing me that had those three babies lived, we could never have gone back to the college and seminary campus for seven years to be equipped for the life to which He had called us. His purpose. And *my* good!

*Dear Lord, hindsight is so great. Thanks for letting me live long enough to see that through the years You really were working all things, especially the devastating ones, for my good*
*—even if I couldn't see it then.*
*In Jesus' precious name, Amen.*

# JOY

*These things we write,*
*so that our joy may be made complete.*
1 John 1:4, NASB

nderstanding the "why" from God produced another gain—unbelievable joy. After those 14 days of living "upside down" in bed, the final verdict from the doctor came—our baby was dead. But this time God came in proportion to my need in a more personal way—just for me. He replaced the loss with *joy.*

I smiled inside at the eager young intern who, at seeing my joy, concluded he had uncovered a then illegal abortion right there in his hospital. His sleuthing intensified as he saw my doctor's name—the obstetrics teacher in that hospital! It was futile to try to explain during the intern's countless cross-examinations that God had turned my loss into joy. He didn't know, couldn't know, how God had come in proportion to my need.

After this "why" explanation from God, complete trust in Him started to come. It was then that His purpose for my whole life began to come into focus. I was gaining through my losses. Although I would not yet articulate that in those exact words until finding them in that poem several years later [see pages 103-104], it was then that *gaining* through *losing* took shape in me. Through the loss of an unborn baby's death.

Oh, how rich I am because God always took my death-losses and turned them into gains—for me and then for others!

*Gaining through losing.* It all came into focus the other day. The wife of the "little boy next door" from Rockford met me in front of the seminary where her husband is now an administrator. She had lost their expected baby in a miscarriage a few days before. I fought back the tears as she said to me, "God brought you into my life for such a day as this."

Has God come in proportion to your need?

*Dear Father, how can I begin to thank You for the incredible joy that you have replaced for my losses since I was twenty-three years old? Thank You for writing in Your Word, the Bible, that awesome Romans 8:28 for me—so that I could know real joy from You. In Jesus' name, Amen.*

# To Die Is Gain?

*For to me to live is Christ, and to die is gain.*
Philipians 1:21, KJV

o die is gain? The person is gone—forever. Everything that belonged to the deceased—money, property, family, life itself—all lost to him. But isn't it from our earthly perspective that we measure the losses of our loved ones? In our grief it is difficult for us to see that death is all gain for one who has died in the Lord. Paul wrote:

*For to me to live is Christ, and to die is gain (Phil. 1:21).*

This is our assurance, and we can cry with Paul, "O death, where is thy sting? O grave, where is thy victory?" (1 Cor. 15:55). My sister expressed it this way in a thank you note for flowers sent for her saintly father-in-law's funeral: "Grandpa would have been 89 today. He can celebrate on a far higher plane than he could have with cake and candles!" If our loved ones have known Christ as Savior and Lord, then we can have absolute assurance that for them all is gain.

It is *our* sense of loss that makes us want them to stay here with us—not theirs.

But death *is* loss—crushing, numbing loss.

As we stepped into the mortuary right after my brother Bud's death, Mother momentarily froze in her steps just inside the entry door. Gone! Then, bracing ourselves, we walked stoically into the room marked, "Mr. Luhman." As we stood by his casket, I took my frail little mother in my arms and, pressing my cheek against her white hair, whispered, "Mother, this is the ultimate Romans 8:28!" That had been our secret—ours through the years when life had crumbled and collapsed around us. When by earthly standards life wasn't worth living, we could always with a squeeze of the hand or an understanding glance whisper, "Romans 8:28." God working everything together for *our good.*

But that day this concept took on a new dimension—God working all things for *Bud's* good. Yet, somehow it was more than good. It was triumph! What was our *loss* was Bud's *gain.* Yes, we were gazing down at "to die is *gain."*

*Dear Heavenly Father, what an awesome life-changing privilege to be able to know that, in spite of all ties severed on earth, our loved one at death has gained the ultimate triumph—life forever in heaven.*
*In Jesus' victorious name, Amen.*

# THEIR GAIN—
## PARADISE WITH JESUS

*Behold, I see the heavens opened, and the Son of man
standing at the right hand of God.*
Acts 7:56, KJV

uring the loss of a loved one, we can start the
process of turning it into our gain by lifting
our eyes, as our loved ones have, to their gain—
Jesus. Frequently, we hear of the glorious experience
of a Christian glimpsing heaven during the dying
process. It happened to Stephen. He saw Jesus—not
only ready to receive him when he drew his last
breath, but also lifting him out of the misery of the
lethal stones that were snuffing out his earthly life.

> *But he, being full of the Holy Ghost, looked up
> steadfastly into heaven, and saw the glory of God,
> and Jesus standing on the right hand of God. And
> said, "Behold, I see the heavens opened, and the
> Son of man standing at he right hand of God"
> (Acts 7:55-56).*

Transcending the stoning, Stephen transfixed his
eyes on his Lord—Jesus—in heaven. Then there is
recorded for us one of the most remarkable conver-

sations ever heard on earth. Stephen, as he was being stoned, asked Jesus to receive his spirit. His last words were addressed, not to those humans around him, but to the Lord. Stephen knelt and cried with a loud voice, "Lord, lay not this sin to their charge" (Acts 7:60). Jesus was so real at the time of death that Stephen actually talked to Him.

To have communication with Jesus seems to be the privilege of many of God's children while they are dying. My stepfather told me that one morning his first wife, who was dying of breast cancer, told him that she would die that night—and she did. Her doctors and nurses had said, "She is not that close to death yet." But she knew that she was. Then he smiled as he reminisced: "Her face absolutely glowed that morning as she told me. And it glowed all that day." She had heard from her beckoning Lord, her Jesus!

*Dear Jesus, thank You that in dying You paid the price for my sins, making me eligible for eternity with You. But, most of all, thank You that You will be waiting to personally usher us into Your presence. In our loving Lord's name, Amen.*

# PREPARED TO GAIN ETERNALLY

*"Today shalt thou be with me in paradise."*
Luke 23:43, KJV

any parents agonize over their children's readiness to meet God at death. For 30 years Mother had prayed every day for God to bring her boy back to Himself. The rest of us had prayed too. We interceded through all those years of his rebellion against God, and when he finally had said, "There is no God."

For two years Mother prayed, "God, do anything You have to do to bring Bud back to Yourself." Then the accident. The car was traveling 50 mph and my brother, a pedestrian, was hit. Tubes, pumps, and intensive care were all that lay between him and eternity when our family arrived at the hospital. And Mother sobbed, "Is it *my* fault—for praying that way to God?"

The next morning Mother and I were allowed to visit him. I bent over his seemingly lifeless body and said deliberately, "Bud, . . . God . . . loves . . . you." The God he declared didn't exist! But at that moment there came the first flicker of life. Bud stirred. The minutes ticked by. I waited, fearing that any sudden shock would push him, unprepared, into eternity. But in desperation I knew I had to say something more.

"Bud . . . can . . . you . . . trust . . . Jesus . . . today?" I intoned. Suddenly he was awake, and through the tubes and hardware, he grinned at me and mouthed a strong affirmative, "Uh, huh!"

God gave him over two more years to live, and it was again Mother who took care of him when the doctors could do no more. In the last couple hours of his life here on earth, he reviewed for her his whole spiritual journey with God since he was a boy—loving Him, leaving Him, denying Him, and then returning to Him. "I'll see you in heaven, Mother." With that he went to sleep. Just two hours later, with a violent lunge, he found himself in that heaven. Loss for her—but indescribable gain for him!

"Today shalt thou be with me in paradise," promised Jesus (see Luke 23:43)—to the dying thief on that other cross—and to my brother. What a *gain* suddenly to be transported into heaven to be with Jesus, the very Son of God!

*Dear Jesus, thank You that when my mother was ushered into heaven by You, her only son was waiting for her. What an awesome gain it will be for us down here on earth when, one by one, You transport us to heaven to be with them—and You.*
*In Your wonderful name, Amen.*

# REIGNING WITH JESUS

*But I would not have you to be ignorant, brethren,*
*concerning them which are asleep, that you sorrow*
*not, even as others who have no hope.*
1 Thessalonians 4:13, KJV

ust one month after my brother's funeral, I wanted to call Mother early since it was her first Mother's Day without one of her children. I had visions of her being in deep despair and grief.

But I was amazed when she answered the phone. She cheerily said, "Hello," and seemed so on top of it all.

Apprehensively I asked, "How are you, Mother?"

Then she answered with, "What greater privilege could there be for a mother than to have one of her children in heaven on Mother's Day?" Yes, there continues to be that hurting void in her life. Yet it is always transcended by *where* he is.

How good it is to watch the beautiful thing which is happening at many Christian funerals these days—turning an almost pagan ritual of despair to a victory celebration for the one who has experienced final, glorious gain—heaven. With Jesus, who, by His own death, secured once and for all the fact that dying *can be gain.*

We were not created by God to die—to have our bodies separated from our souls. This was the result of the fall in the Garden of Eden. But God took away death's terror by making death itself the doorway to heaven.

"O, death, where is thy sting? O grave, where is thy victory? . . . But thanks be to God who giveth us the victory through our Lord Jesus Christ." For many years I have asked my family to have the "Hallelujah Chorus" from Handel's *Messiah* sung at my funeral. Turning their *loss* into *gain* by lifting their eyes and hearts to the glorious place of total and eternal joy— reigning with Jesus!

Culmination? No! Coronation!

*Dear Lord, while we are living in a world seemingly getting more and more evil, how wonderful to know it is just temporary. Our eons of eternity will be spent in total joy with You! In Jesus' precious name, Amen.*

## FORSAKEN

*I will never desert you, nor will I ever forsake you. . . .*
*The LORD is my helper, I will not be afraid.*
*What shall man do to me?*
Hebrews 13:5-6, NASB

s separation by death the only cause of aloneness? Is there a *loss* of human association that
can be even more difficult to bear than death?

In death there is generally the factor of God's sovereignty. We can find solace in the fact that the ultimate controlling force in death is God. Whether we
accept it or blame Him, we still hide behind the
knowledge that, after all, death is really beyond our
control.

But not so when a loved one deliberately chooses
to sever or replace a relationship. Forsaken! This can
sometimes be a far more devastating loss than death.

When a loved one severs a relationship—especially
when it leads to that final loss, divorce—the wound
can be even deeper than death. Whereas in death the
departed one (if in Christ) gains, in divorce both lose.
They lose the security, the oneness given them by
God in marriage. They both lose a stockpile of shared
experiences, hopes, dreams, and possessions. And

the innocent party (years of counseling heartbroken spouses have led me to believe there are some of those) not only suffers the same losses as the one who leaves, but frequently loses self-esteem, and goes on living in guilt and remorse. Guilt because of a sense of failure; remorse because things might have been done differently.

What can possibly be *gained* in this ruptured relationship? Except for those horrible cases involving physical or emotional brutality, is there any hope of coming through this kind of *losing* and actually *gaining*?

I have listened, astounded, as the forsaken ones have told me how God has met them at the point of their devastatingly deep needs. How He has taken over and filled the void with Himself. How they have been able not only to cope, but actually to find something given to them by God to replace the lost relationship.

This does not suggest that it is God's will that a marriage be broken. "What therefore God hath joined together let not man put asunder" (Mark 10:9). But God can pick up the pieces of the shattered life and put them together, so bound with His love, that the scar tissue is stronger than the natural flesh.

*Dear Heavenly Father, it is so wonderful to have seen so many who have been forsaken by their mates and then have the devastating void filled by You. Please come to all Your children who need You like that right now. In Jesus' love, Amen.*

## Misplaced Expectations

*. . . to know that this love that surpasses knowledge—*
*that you may be filled to the measure*
*of all the fullness of God.*
Ephesians 3:19, NIV

 erhaps the reason so many are seeking alternative human companionship is because they have never found an adequate source to fulfill their needs. They may be expecting more than God intended from a human being. Should we expect anyone to be able to meet all of our needs at all times?

One woman said to me, "When my husband and I were first married, I had just found Christ and didn't fully understand what a Christian really was. I was dependent on my husband for all my needs, and he was just like God to me. Then I would criticize him because he didn't measure up to what I thought a Christian should be. My husband is head of our house, but he is not infallible. How much better it is to discover that we can't expect our husbands to be what only God can be."

Then she went on. "God is sufficient for every need that I *want* Him to be sufficient for. Sometimes we just want to feel sorry for ourselves, to nurse along the feeling that my mate 'doesn't understand my needs,' thus justifying the turning to forbidden ones. But God *is* sufficient for every need."

I too have found that not being understood, not having my needs fulfilled, involves a very difficult kind of loneliness, a sense of being forsaken. But in this loss I have found an overwhelming *gain.*

When a parent, a friend, a roommate, or a spouse cannot or will not meet my needs, it is really an advantage. For this has always driven me to the One who not only understands but cares. To the One who is always there to meet my needs. I have learned that a fantastic relationship with the Lord only develops in this kind of loneliness. What a privilege! The *loss* produces a *gain* that no human companionship could ever match. Fellowship with the Lord—who always understands. And bids us come to Him!

*Dear God, teach me never to expect* anyone *except You to be able to meet all my needs. Thank You, Lord, for the fantastic companionship You have ready for Your children when humans fail us. In Jesus' name, Amen.*

# The Bidding One or Forbidden One?

*My God shall supply all your needs.*
Philippians 4:19, KJV

any people who are alone have told me about their beautiful, spiritual "love affair" with Jesus—being filled in the pure and holy love of their Savior. But all love affairs are not holy. It is possible in loneliness to turn not to the Bidding One, but to a forbidden one to find human companionship.

An unmarried woman confided to me, "I'm in love with a man I can never have." Then hesitatingly she asked, "Will God really supply *all* my needs?"

"Yes, He will," I quickly answered, thinking she was referring to Philippians 4:19: "My God shall supply all your needs. . . ."

"No," she explained, "I mean *all* my needs," and suddenly I realized she was talking about her sexual needs.

Then I said, "To find sexual fulfillment from forbidden fruit is *never* God's way of meeting our needs. That is Satan's way. Ask God to forgive you and be done with that relationship."

Jesus said that the Father knows what we have

need of before we ever ask Him (Matt. 6:8). So He knows our needs, and in Philippians 4:19 we are told that the *person* supplying them is God. And how many of them? All!

How does God supply *all* these needs? I vividly recall the indescribable loneliness I felt as a young wife, married just 11 months, when my husband was called into the service during World War II. My invalid dad would sit by the radio and keep track of the B-17 bombing raids in Europe announced on the daily news. No matter how recent a letter I had received from my pilot-husband, I always wondered whether I was a wife or a widow. I was never really sure till the day I read the cable that said, "Missions all done. Coming home. Love, Chris."

I found that God would and did supply all my needs in that aching loneliness. The secret? He took away those needs and gave me complete satisfaction when I immersed myself in Jesus. In His Word. In talking to Him. Receiving support, comfort, and guidance from Him. And immersing myself in serving Him. He was always there—loving me, occupying my time, controlling my emotions. Supplying *all* my needs.

*Dear Jesus, thank You that You fulfill our needs, but not in the human ways we expect or think we deserve. Your ways are always pure, holy—and absolutely sufficient! Thanks, Jesus! In Your wonderful name, Amen.*

# INNOCENT VICTIMS—FORSAKEN

*"I will not leave you comfortless: I will come to you."*
John 14:18, KJV

The greatest tragedy resulting from a broken home is its effect on children. Whether the loss has been precipitated by deliberate separation on the part of the parents or by God through death, the children seem to experience the greatest loss.

I was reminded of Kum Ja, a beautiful little girl with an angelic voice who was a member of the Korean Orphan's Choir when they sang in our church years ago. Today she is a citizen of the United States and is working on her doctorate degree in music.

She shared with me some of her experiences as an orphan in Korea. With no one to care for her, she ate out of garbage cans and slept in doorways. You can imagine how startled I was when she said to me, "But I am one of the most privileged people in the world. With no human source of support, I had learned by the time I was two years of age, that God would take care of me. I came to know Him in a way few people ever have the chance to know Him. I am indeed a privileged person to have been deprived of all human relationships when just a little child, for I came to know Him in such a wonderful way."

Astounding? Yes. In her indescribable need, God had met her in a way rarely experienced by most people. Abandoned? Certainly, although not intentionally by her deceased parents. But in her little mind—*forsaken*. Forsaken—until the God of the universe came in that fantastic way that almost defies human comprehension.

Jesus explained to His followers that He would not leave them comfortless when He left them (bodily) but would come to them (John 14:18). The meaning of the word *comfortless* in the original Greek surprised me: "forsaken and abandoned ones . . . *orphans*"!

"I will come to them." He promised!

Children have a keen sense of being forsaken and abandoned when they are deprived of one or both parents. Do we lead them to the God who understands, fills the void, and supplies their needs? Have we given them the assurance that there is one Friend who will never, never leave them nor forsake them?

*Dear Jesus, please help me to feel what forsaken and abandoned children feel. Forgive me for not caring enough. Help me to bring them not just human help, but You, Jesus—who alone can fill the void in their lives. In Your compassionate name, Amen.*

## NOTHING CAN SEPARATE

*[Nothing] shall be able to separate us from the love of*
*God, which is in Christ Jesus our Lord.*
Romans 8:39, KJV

here are reasons for feeling forsaken in addition to death and broken homes. At times, security, acceptance, and fellowship are wrenched from us by our own actions or by the actions of others. But the Bible offers assurance for these times, too:

*Who shall separate us from the love of Christ?* Shall tribulation, or distress, or persecution, or famine, or nakedness, or peril, or sword? . . . Nay, in all these things we are more than conquerors through Him that loved us. For I am persuaded, that neither death, nor life, nor angels, nor principalities, nor powers, nor things present, nor things to come, nor height, nor depth, nor any other creature, shall be able to *separate us from the love of God,* which is in Christ Jesus, our Lord (Rom. 8:35, 37-39, italics added).

Kari Malcom, a daughter of missionary parents in China, told me of her feelings when she found herself in a Japanese concentration camp while still in high school. She had lost her father and all her material possessions. "But my hardest loss came," she explained, "in a break with my close girlfriends. We daily met for prayer, asking God to take us out of that concentration camp. But God eventually convicted me of that prayer," she said, "and finally I could go to those meetings no more."

Her girlfriends became angry with her and ostracized her. She was excluded—emotionally and physically— and forsaken by her close friends in a hostile, friendless environment—a concentration camp.

The reason she had stopped asking God to release them from the concentration camp was that she had discovered a different prayer: "God, I will stay in prison the rest of my life *if I may only know You.*" Yes, she had found a relationship deeper than one with a peer group. She had found a Friend closer than any of her earthly friends. Then she beamed at me and declared, "Since praying that prayer, all that matters is my relationship to God." Nothing could separate her from her God!

*Dear God, it is overwhleming to realize that there is no one or no thing that can separate us from Your love. Our relationship with You always will transcend all others—loved immovably by You.*
*In Jesus' name, Amen.*

## JESUS UNDERSTANDS

*We do not have a high priest who is unable to
sympathize with our weaknesses. . . .*
Hebrews 4:15, NIV

esus knows what it is like to be misunderstood and excluded by friends.

When He returned to Galilee with His fame spread
through all the regions round about, Jesus found it to
be quite different in His hometown, Nazareth. He
stood up to read and preach in the synagogue, and
His childhood friends recognized Him only as member of a local family, not as the Son of God. They
"were filled with wrath, and rose up, and thrust Him
out of the city, and led Him unto the brow of the hill
whereon their [also His] city was built, that they
might cast Him down headlong" (Luke 4:28-29).
Jesus was more than emotionally ostracized by His
childhood friends. He actually fled for His life as
they violently forced Him toward a cliff so that they
could push Him over to His death.

This past summer I heard a prominent Russian
pastor speak just two months after being released
from a slave labor camp. He said, "I had to wear red
stripes because I was considered the most dangerous

kind of criminal in the camp. I was not allowed to fellowship with other prisoners. If the guards saw me talking to others, they would put us in separate barracks. Other prisoners were brainwashed against me as I was declared to be worse than a murderer."

But then he told us that no matter how segregated he was, he always had great fellowship with his Lord. His captors could not take that away from him! Separated—but not from God's love and companionship!

Jesus also understands what it is like to be ostracized by those in authority. Throughout His public ministry, there was a running battle between Jesus and the religious leaders of His day. They called Him a liar, attempted to stone Him, took counsel together to put Him to death, delivered Him to the civil authorities unjustly—until they finally cried to Pilate, "Crucify Him, crucify Him" (Matt. 27:22-23). Ostracized by religious leaders—but not separated from His Father's love.

*Dear Jesus, whenever I am misunderstood and even kept on the outside of a religious group, You know how it hurts—because You paid a much higher price than I ever will. Thank You, dearest Jesus.*
*In Your precious name, Amen.*

# SINGLENESS

*I am not alone, because the Father is with me."*
John 16:32, KJV

linging to the promise that the Lord never leaves us is not always easy. Feeling forsaken for all those who might have, could have, or wanted to marry us can be difficult—especially when feeling forsaken *for* another—the one they did marry.

Does the Lord Jesus understand singleness? Did He feel that kind of loneliness? Did He feel cheated? *Or,* because He was without a mate, did He experience His Father in heaven being with Him in a special way—as He glorified His Father and did His Father's will in all things?

A well-known Christian author and radio personality who has never married told me many years ago that she found singleness to be a blessing. She had discovered in her aloneness that she and God had a very special relationship. When she had said that, inside me a slight sneer raised its ugly head as I piously smiled and strained to agree with her. In my youthful inexperience, I thought she was only trying to justify her singleness.

Then I remarked a little smugly, "*I* have the best of *both* worlds. I have the privilege of having a husband *and* knowing God that way." But did I? Perhaps those of us who live in the security of mates who comfort, love, and provide necessities for us have never had the privilege of depending as completely on God— knowing Him to that depth. Had she merely become resigned to the state in which she found herself, *or* had she really found a relationship with God that only comes in aloneness? Since God understands our need for companionship—He created us that way— how natural and understandable that He will fill that need with Himself.

Jesus never married, yet at the end of His life He could say, "I am not alone, because the Father is with me" (John 16:32). Could you say the same thing?

*Dear Father in heaven, I am praying for all of my dear friends who never have married. Please press deeply in their hearts that the most important and perfect person ever to live on Planet Earth was single—You, dear Jesus. In Your name, Amen.*

# JESUS WAS FORSAKEN

*"My God, my God, why hast thou forsaken me?"*
Matthew 27:46, KJV

esus understood being alone—forsaken. Toward the end of His ministry on earth, the huge crowds that wanted to make Him their king turned against Him—and followed Him no more. As He entered Jerusalem for the last time, they sang, "Hosanna in the highest" and instituted the first Palm Sunday by strewing palm branches at His feet. But by Thursday night, the forsaking had begun. His disciples, His closest friends, betrayed, denied, and forsook Him in His hour of great need. There were no familiar, friendly faces, no trusting supporters at His trial—not one!

But Jesus knew that He would be forsaken. He had already told them, "[You] shall leave me alone." But He added, "Yet I am not alone, because the Father is with me" (John 16:32). That fact is also true for all of us as followers of Jesus—we are never alone for the Father is with us.

But it was while suffering on His cross that Jesus had a sense of being forsaken that will never be experienced by any true follower of His. The Father was always with Him—until that excruciating moment when Jesus cried with a loud voice, "My God, my God, why hast thou forsaken me?" (Matt. 27:46). As Jesus hung on that cross, the Father had to turn from His Son in order that the Son could experience and bear our sins in His death.

That forsakenness will never be ours. We who deserve to be forsaken by the holy God will never be—because Jesus, who had never sinned, undeservedly bore that sin for us. We will never be forsaken as Jesus was—for us.

*My dear Jesus, my heart is broken that, while we Christians will never be forsaken by the Father, You were. And it was all our fault. When You were taking our sins upon Yourself, You were forsaken by the Father so that we, cleansed, would never have to be. Thank You, Jesus! In Your precious name, Amen.*

## Don't Waste Your Forsakenness

*As the deer pants for streams of water,*
*so my soul pants for you, O God.*
Psalm 42:1, KJV

orsakenness comes in degrees—from the shattering of death or divorce to the first day of kindergarten. But don't waste one of them! Practice experiencing all of God's unchanging steadfastness in the little bumps and in the enormous disasters so that, no matter what kind of forsakenness engulfs you, you can experience what Paul did. Join him in his absolute assurance, born experientially out of every conceivable loss, through temporal adversities and spiritual conflicts, summing up with almost ecstatic confidence: "[Nothing] shall be able to separate us from the love of God, which is in Christ Jesus our Lord" (Rom. 8:39).

Confidence *gained* through our *losses!*

One summer evening, Chris, his sister Shirley, and I were hiking along the shore of Lake Michigan. We were exhilarated and chatting happily when suddenly my weak leg started to drag, making marks in the sand. There was only one thing for me to do—turn back. I felt a twinge of forsakenness as I turned to walk to the cottage—alone. But as I saw only the lake and the sand stretching out in front of me—no other person in sight—my heart suddenly leaped within me. "I love You, God. Just You, God. What a great feeling. All alone with *You.*"

I recalled how I felt just before Chris and I were married, when there were places it was not proper to be alone with Chris. And that insatiable thirst to be alone with him. "This thirst is how I feel about You, God."

I hiked, my heart soaring. Then I sat on the sand, just so the lapping waves missed my feet, and watched the progressing sunset. I hugged my knees. A thrill tingled down my spine. Not forsaken! Not alone! God!

Don't waste your losses!

*Dear God, although You are Father to all the believers on earth, because You are God, You come apart to be alone with just me. Thank You, Father, for the wonderful thrill when You do. In Jesus' name, Amen.*

## LOSING MY RIGHT TO RUN MY OWN LIFE

*"Therefore let all Israel be assured of this: God has made this Jesus, whom you crucified, both Lord and Christ."*
Acts 2:26, NIV

o matter how important the loved one whom I have lost in separation or death may have been to me, there is one other human possession who always wants to be Number One—the one I cling to most dearly and struggle so hard to keep—myself. It is the "I" in my life, the "I" that I strive the hardest to protect and nourish.

Even in dealing with losses by death, I have clung to this prized possession—protecting, pampering, and preserving this "I." At times it becomes very difficult to give up the "rights" of this prized possession. The rights I feel are legally, rightfully mine.

How like William Ernest Henley we are in forcefully asserting, if not aloud to others, at least in the secret recesses of our hearts the words of his *Invictus:*

*It matters not how straight the gate*
*How charged with punishments the scroll,*
*I am the master of my fate;*
*I am the captain of my soul.*

(Arthur Quiller-Couch, ed., *The Oxford Book of*

*English Verse*, Oxford University Press.)

We feel we have the right to sovereignty over our own lives. But do we? Is this, or has it ever been, the right of the Christian? Is it the difference between knowing Christ only as Savior or as both Savior and Lord?

Thomas, on seeing the wounds in the risen Savior's hands, immediately enjoined the disciples' familiar name for Jesus, "Lord," with the absolute title of deity: "My Lord *and* my God." After that there is no record of that Greek word *kurios* ever being used by believers in addressing any but God and the Lord Jesus. It was a term they used interchangeably with God—and Jesus. (See William E. Vine's *Expository Dictionary of New Testament Words*, Revell, Volume III, p. 17.) Sovereignty—not I but Jesus.

Peter, after the resurrection and ascension of Jesus, told those who had crucified Him that God had made Jesus both Lord and Christ (Acts 2:36). It was because of that resurrection, he explained, that the full significance of the title *Lord* could be understood. Lord—having power and authority.

*Dear Jesus, You are not just my Savior but my Lord and my God. I eagerly bow before You. You are number one in my life! Help me to give You total control of my life. In Your name, Amen.*

# KEEPING STATISTICS OF EVIL

*"Love keeps no score of wrongs."*
1 Corinthians 13:5, NEB

re you aware that each of us have an internal "bookkeeping" system? We have one column in the ledger where we record the good things which happen to us, and another where we keep track of the wrongs leveled against us. Year after year these accumulated statistics tip the balance one way or the other. The side outweighing the other has a strong effect on our whole being. If it is the "bad" side, it can affect us adversely.

I heard of a woman who actually has a little book with a page for each acquaintance. She makes an entry each time they say or do something against her. Then when she comes to a predetermined number, she draws a dark diagonal line across that page—slashing her off her list of friends! Statistics of evil.

But forgiving does a strange thing to the forgiver's column of hurts. It wipes clean the evil statistics which have been hoarded in the internal ledgers. In 1 Corinthians 13:5, that great love chapter, we read, "Love keeps no score of wrongs" (1 Cor. 13:5, NEB). In other words, as in the Phillips translation, "It does not keep account of evil."

It is so easy to compile, keep adding up, the score of wrongs committed against us. We poke them deep down inside ourselves, layer upon layer, instead of forgiving and being done with them. Doctors tell us we actually can make ourselves ill when we push hurts and resentments deeper and deeper inside. These attitudes eat away at us from the *inside out,* causing emotional and sometimes physical ills.

We may feel there is a personal gain in the satisfaction we derive from exercising our "right" to refuse to give up our angry, negative, accusing, wounded spirit. But in reality just the opposite is true. We are the *losers.* The emotional and physical gains come when we take our spiritual eraser and wipe the ledger clean—by forgiving.

*Dear God, help me realize that I am the loser when I keep track of the wrongs done against me. Give me the strength to sincerely forgive those who have hurt me and erase all those collected hurts eating away at me. In Jesus' name, Amen.*

# NO STATISTICS OF EVIL

*"Be ye kind to one another, tenderhearted,*
*forgiving one another."*
Ephesians 4:32, KJV

n added dimension to a clean internal ledger is: *Don't let evil statistics accumulate in the first place.*

One of the most strikingly beautiful people I have ever seen is a 60-year-old fellow speaker whom I met at a retreat. After we had prayed through our exercise of forgiving someone, she explained to me, "Evelyn, I honestly could not think of anyone to forgive. You see, for years I have practiced forgiving immediately. Never holding anything against anybody."

Frequently, people try to tell me that, but their faces contradict their words. But the radiant glow on her face and the spring in her step attested to the truth of her statement. Here was a beaming, radiant woman in her 60th year who was living proof of what happens to a face that through the years has not compiled statistics of evil. Preventative medicine! Handsome men and beautiful women!

I've heard it said that we are responsible for our own faces after 40. The lines and sags distribute themselves according to the expressions we have exercised through the years. No matter how perfect the features, facial beauty disappears from the countenance harboring the "right" to be touchy, to hold onto grudges or an accusing spirit. The most beautiful features can never compensate for a mouth pursed with resentment, and with corners drooped in touchiness; eyes narrowed with vindictiveness—surfacing from their statistics of evil column. But the plainest features somehow come alive with a radiance and beauty when they exude not peevishness, anger, and resentment, but love—unconditional love. *Gaining* through losing the right to harbor an unforgiving spirit.

Modern medicine is stressing not just healing for existing ills, but preventive measures as well. But the formula has existed for 20 centuries in the Bible. In all my Bibles I have used since I was 18 years old, I have underlined Ephesians 4:32, "Be ye kind to one another, tenderhearted, forgiving one another." Here was God giving *me* a prescription for preventive medicine through all those years.

*Dear Lord, I really want that kind of beauty radiating from me. Keep me ever applying Your prescription of kindness, tenderheartedness, and forgiveness so I will have it. In Jesus' beautiful name, Amen.*

## Marriages Mended by Forgiveness

*Bear with each other and forgive whatever grievances*
*you may have against one another.*
*Forgive as the Lord forgave you.*
Colossians 3:13, NIV

 arriages are frequently mended by the simple act of forgiving. After my plane landed in the East for a seminar, the pastor's wife briefed me on their church's prayer chains and groups. "We've had a miracle take place. If so-and-so tells you her story, listen. It's a miracle!"

At lunch I was sitting next to so-and-so who told me, "My husband was fooling around with his secretary and decided to leave the children and me to live in a motel, so he could spend his nights with her. While he was packing his bag, I tucked in a Bible, even though he never reads one. Every day the children and I prayed for our daddy, and every week prayer chains and groups at church prayed, too. Then one Saturday after he had been gone several months, I read in my morning devotions:

*The Lord hath been witness between thee and the*
*wife of thy youth, against whom thou hast dealt*

*treacherously: yet is she thy companion, and the wife of thy covenant. And did not he make one? . . . Therefore take heed to your spirit, and let none deal treacherously against the wife of his youth* (Mal. 2:14-15).

Her eyes narrowed with resolve as she continued: "'Hey,' I said to myself, 'I'm the wife of his youth. He doesn't have a right to treat me like this,' And I began to pray, 'Lord, send him to Malachi 2.' *Oh, what a stupid prayer. He never reads the Bible.*

"But *that very night* my husband came to his senses. Realizing what he had done to his children and me, he started pacing the floor and was contemplating suicide. Then he flung himself on the bed with his head hanging slightly over his partially unpacked suitcase. And there in plain view, out from the midst of the clothes, was—yes, that Bible.

"He grabbed it and, in desperation, just opened it at random. Yes—to Malachi 2! He read those words, ran home, and begged us to forgive him, which, of course, we so eagerly did." Another family together again.

*Dear Father, the polls are reporting that right now the divorce rate among people calling themselves Christians is a little higher than non-Christians. O God, I pray that You would show those feuding couples Your divine secret for reconciliation—forgiving! In the name of the Great Forgiver, Jesus, Amen.*

## REVENGE—FORGIVENESS

*"Pray for them which despitefully use you,*
*and persecute you."*
Matthew 5:44, KJV

 stately black woman, a clinical professor of surgery in a large Southern hospital, was addressing us in the Bahamas. I listened carefully as she described the racial hatred and sex discrimination through which she had to claw and crawl to become the first black woman surgeon in the South. Then with a beautiful, radiant smile, she said, "But no revenge is so complete as forgiveness."

Revenge—forgiveness? I pondered that puzzling statement for days. What did she mean? Not revenge by her fabulous success story? Not by showing them that she could do it? How had she *won by forgiving?* She had wiped all the resentment and bitterness out of her heart—in the act of forgiving! She was changed. She was released. She was the beautiful, radiant surgeon—transcending and living victoriously above all their hurtful acts. No statistics of evil left to eat away at her from within. Her ultimate victory—forgiving!

Jesus demonstrated this kind of victory on the

cross. Triumph over His enemies came not only when He was raised from the dead. Oh, no. It also came *during* the physical torture and spiritual anguish. Victory came as Jesus, while suffering excruciating physical and spiritual agony on the cross, practiced His own admonition to us: "Pray for them which despitefully use you, and persecute you" (Matt. 5:44). The complete victory was in His prayer, "Father, *forgive them;* for they know not what they do" (Luke 23:34, italics added). Why? Because *they were no longer His enemies.* He was Victor!

*Dearest Jesus, when You forgave those who were crucifying You, You were the victor. Press this truth deeply in my heart so that I too can be victorious, released, and a winner when I forgive. Thanks for being such an awesome example, dear Jesus.*
*In Your name, Amen.*

# WHY DO SO FEW PRAY?

*You have not because you ask not.*
James 4:2, NASB

 hile being interviewed by a Christian counselor in California, I was asked a very profound question. "Evelyn, since all Christians know that there is power and guidance in prayer, why is it so few of them really pray diligently and fervently?"

"There are many reasons," I answered, "but one of the main ones is pride. It is hard to admit we need help or that our way of doing it may not be right. In fact," I continued, "deep down in their hearts many Christians are saying 'I can do it myself, God!'"

Also, many people glibly say, "All's well that ends well." But this is just wishful thinking and not true if they haven't included God in their human handling of circumstances and events.

How foolish it is to depend on our inadequate, limited, and biased opinions and wisdom—when we don't pray.

How foolish to deprive our families of all that fantastic good—when we don't pray.

How surprising that Christian families grope and

stumble and sometimes break up—because they have not bothered to call for God's help.

The Bible clearly says one of the main reasons we don't have solutions to our family problems is that we have not asked God for them. We have not prayed. "You have not because you ask not" (James 4:2, NASB).

*But when we do pray, God releases His divine power into the lives of our family members.*

Our prayer groups at our church joined a devastated mother and father praying persistently for their son. He had left his family's Christian lifestyle for one of organized crime. It took years of their praying—and ours. But prayer did work. Today he is the father of a fine family and on the board of a good church.

Another family had a daughter who was breaking their hearts. She rebelled at the Christian leadership lifestyle of her parents and many times refused to go to high school. She ended up running from the family, on drugs, and in a very godless lifestyle. But our prayer groups joined her praying parents also— praying almost daily. And now she and her husband have a successful ministry in Hollywood reaching those in the movie industry for Jesus.

Are you praying for your family?

*Dear Lord, I don't understand why You usually chose to wait for me to ask before You would act, but You did. Forgive me for all the times I have been too proud to ask for Your help—and missed Your help. In Jesus' name, Amen.*

## OUR FAMILY'S LIFESTYLE

*Pray without ceasing.*
1 Thessalonians 5:17, NASB

od literally has run my family through prayer. Our multiple family problems have kept us on our faces before God. Many, many times our dependence on Him has been our means of survival. But God has been in control of our family decisions, relationships, joys, and trials. In these fifty years of marriage, our family literally has had a spontaneous lifestyle of prayer.

Since becoming a mother and a grandmother, I know what the Bible means by the admonition "Pray without ceasing" (1 Thes. 5:17, NASB).

It is not just the bedtime praying of my husband and me which always includes each of the family members. Not just my daily morning devotions when I always intercede fervently for my family members. It is not just the formal times we pray together for each other, or the spontaneous quick prayers when a need suddenly arises. No, family prayer is the lifestyle of our family—independently and with each other.

Also, each of my family members does not get the same amount or intensity of prayer each day. Family prayers are not a formal listing of each member in a prayer diary to be dutifully or even perfunctorily prayed through. *No, the time spent on each is directly in proportion to the individual's need that day.*

Prayer is sweeping my grandchildren into my arms when they are afraid—thanking God with them for His protection. It is pacing with an infant granddaughter with colic, breathing a continuous prayer for relief. It is including God's comfort along with the bandage on a skinned knee. It is asking for God's healing as a hand is laid comfortingly on a sick tummy or fevered forehead—or for a husband during surgery. It is clinging in faith to God while pacing the floor with the unwashed grandbaby while the surgeons race to save a daughter's life. It is agonizing through a sleepless night for a wayward child.

Prayer in our family isn't something we do occasionally; it is a way of life. *A life lived moment by moment with the most important member of our family—the God of the universe.*

God is longing to be the most important member of your family too.

*Dear Father in heaven, thank You that as a family we have been able to bring all our many earthly problems to You. Oh how many little inconveniences and unbelievable burdens have been lifted, not because You necessarily healed or removed them, but because You took over. Thanks, dear Father. In Jesus' name, Amen.*

## Prayer Acknowledges God
## as Director of Our Families

*Trust in the Lord with all your heart, and lean not on your own understanding. In all thy ways acknowledge Him, and He will direct your paths.*

Proverbs 3:5-6, KJV

 have had special days that I waited in prayer on God for Scripture verses of guidance. For example, back in our pastorate time in Rockford, God would give me the same New Year's Scripture year after year—Proverbs 3:5-6.

At first I was thrilled at knowing He wanted to direct me and my family the next year, and enthusiastically practiced letting Him do it. But as the years passed, and He kept giving me the same Scripture, I became impatient. Was God in a rut? Or had He run out of new ideas for me?

But now I realize that this was a very deliberate repetition, reinforcing the greatest lesson of my life: *If I DON'T lean on my own understanding, and if I DO trust in Him, and if in all my ways I DO acknowledge Him—then, and only then, will God direct my own and our family's paths.*

And how do I acknowledge Him? By running my life by prayer. Depending on Him instead of myself.

I have found this guidance as precise, tangible, definite, and accurate as the star of Bethlehem leading the magi to the Christ Child (Matt. 2:9). When they left Herod, the star appeared again very clearly to them and directed them to the Child. So also with me. The same words apply to my life. *He will direct our paths*—through prayer.

*Dear God, forgive me for the times I thought I knew better than You—and things ended in disaster. But thank You for the incredible guidance You consistently have given me when I asked. Keep me asking! In Jesus' name, Amen.*

# WHEN WE DON'T KNOW HOW TO PRAY

*And in the same way the Spirit also helps our
weakness; for we do not know how to pray as we
should, but the Spirit Himself intercedes for us with
groanings too deep for words; and He who searches
the hearts knows what the mind of the Spirit is,
because He intercedes for the saints
according to the will of God.*

Romans 8:26-27, NASB

 here are those times when we don't know
how to pray for our families. But God has pro-
vided me the solution to that problem. The Father
gave us the Holy Spirit to live in us—who prays to
Him whatever is the Father's will—when we don't
know how to pray.

Our daughter Nancy called recently saying that her
five-year-old Kathy was going through a stage—
arrogant, bossy, and aggressive. Remembering her
older sister's similar attitude and the spiritual war-
fare prayer against Satan that changed her completely, I started to pray the same for Kathy. But somehow
it wasn't right.

Finally, kneeling in the living room, I prayed, "O
Holy Spirit, I don't know how or what to pray for
Kathy. Please take my 'not knowing how to pray as I
ought' to the Father according to His will."

What a relief! The pressure to figure out just what

to pray left me. I knew God knew exactly what Kathy needed—and the Holy Spirit would take my inadequate prayer to the Father exactly according to the Father's will.

Talking to Nancy the next day, I asked about Kathy. A little surprised, she said, "Oh, she seems so much better." I thought, *I wonder how God answered my prayer of not knowing what to pray? Well, I don't need to know as long as God knows—and answers!*

One of the greatest helps to me in my family praying throughout the years has been the burden the Holy Spirit has lifted from me when we don't know how to pray in family situations. When you don't how to pray, ask the Holy Spirit to intercede on your behalf.

*Dear Heavenly Father, thanks that You have not left all the responsibility with me to know how and what to pray. Only You as God could possibly know all the possible outcomes of my prayers. Forgive me for forgetting this so often. In Jesus' name, Amen.*

# No Prayer in the Garden of Eden

*Having therefore, brethren,*
*boldness to enter into the holiest by the blood of Jesus.*
Hebrews 10:19, KJV

od's original plan for Planet Earth did not include prayer. When God put the first family in the Garden of Eden, there was no family prayer. Why? Because Adam and Eve didn't need it. In the first home established on earth, there was perfect one-on-one communication with God. "They heard the sound of the Lord God walking in the garden in the cool of the day" (Gen. 3:8, NASB).

And God carried on direct conversations with them, asking them questions and getting answers from Adam and Eve. They were open, personal friends.

So, why do we need prayer now? Because of *sin*. When Satan brought sin to earth through our first parents, God drove Adam and Eve out of their perfect environment and relationship with Him. Sin destroyed humans' perfect two-way communicating with God.

But God's communicating with people did not cease; it just changed form. He then instituted prayer.

In Genesis 4:26 we read this about Adam and Eve's son Seth: "Then men began to call upon the name of the Lord" (NASB).

And we can see prayer developing throughout the Bible until today when we have communication with the Father restored by Jesus on the cross. Adam and Eve's perfect communion with the Father is available to us, His children. Sweet, unbroken communion has been restored by the shed blood of Jesus Christ—for our families.

*Having therefore, brethren, boldness to enter into the holiest by the blood of Jesus (Heb. 10:19).*

Once we have availed ourselves of that cleansing and redeeming blood of Jesus in salvation, we are eligible for this ideal relationship of unbroken communication with God.

Have you availed yourself of the power of Jesus Christ?

*Dear Father, thank You that since I accepted Jesus at nine years of age, You and I have had this perfect two-way conversation going, I am overwhelmed that You, the omnipotent God of heaven, would make me eligible through Jesus—when I'm so unworthy. Thanks, Lord! In Jesus' name, Amen.*

# Rips and Holes

*Now I exhort you, brethren, by the name of our Lord
Jesus Christ that you all agree, and there be no
divisions among you, but you be made complete in the
same mind and in the same judgment.*
1 Corinthians 1:10, NASB

n all families there are times when a few individuals or even all family members squabble
and have misunderstandings, ripping holes in the
undergirding fabric which has been woven by
prayer. Some holes are easily patched and hardly
affect the strength of the network at all; in some cases
squabbles rip huge gaps in the prayer fabric, causing
a serious disruption in the flow of family prayers or
even a ceasing of praying altogether.

But again, it is the threads of prayer that can mend
the snags and gaping holes in family relationships.
During the Depression of the 1930s, I used to watch
my mother darn socks. She would take one strand of
darning thread and painstakingly weave it back and
forth until what was a hole was stronger than the
original sock. That is how prayer mends a family's
rips and holes.

Through the years, my prayer many, many times
has been in the words of the Apostle Paul's desire for

the family of believers in Corinth when there were quarrels among them:

*Now I exhort you, brethren, by the name of our Lord Jesus Christ that you all agree, and there be no divisions among you, but you be made complete in the same mind and in the same judgment (1 Cor. 1:10, NASB).*

So it is with just one, or perhaps a few family members taking their threads of prayer and patiently, often painstakingly, weaving to mend the family fabric. Sometimes the weaving accomplishes its purpose quickly, but sometimes it takes faithful weaving for years before the rift is mended. Much mending prayer is done in weeping and even agonizing of spirit. But, stitch by stitch, God takes His holy hand and pulls those threads of prayer in place, supernaturally mending those hurtful holes.

*My dear God, what a simple, yet amazingly hard thing it is to pray when there are divisions among us. Please exchange all our grumbling and accusing with prayer for them—and myself—so You can stitch us together with Your holy hands. In Jesus' name, Amen.*

# "How Can I Be Sure, Mother?"

*It is God who works in you to will and to act
according to his good purpose.*
Philippians 2:13, NIV

 t was our daughter Jan's first child. She searched my face for an answer as she asked, "Mother, how can I be absolutely sure Jenna will be saved and go to heaven with me?"

"You can't be absolutely sure, Honey," I replied. "God gave your precious little baby a *free will* just like He gave everybody else on earth."

With tears in her eyes she cried, "What can I do then? Can't I do *anything* about it?"

"Oh, yes, Jan, there are many things you can, and must, do. First you yourself must live your Jesus in front of her every minute. In all you do and say, she must see Jesus living in you. You must teach her the things of God and surround her with music and stories about Jesus. You must keep her encased in a good church family."

This is what Chris and I promised God we would do at the important time of dedicating our infants— but really ourselves—to God.

"But, Jan, by far the most important thing you will

do for her is *pray*. Pray continually that she will find Jesus as soon as she is old enough to understand. Although God gave Jenna a free will, He will move in her heart in proportion to your praying. Pray, pray, pray!

"No one can make that decision for your child, not even you, her parent. Even Jesus didn't assume that authority over anybody. Although Jesus wept over Jerusalem, longing to gather the people to Himself, they would not. Although many of those He was weeping over were born into Jewish families, they chose not to follow Jesus. Nothing you can do, Jan, will guarantee that Jenna will go to heaven. That is strictly a personal decision every person must make—no matter who their parents are or what ritual or rite of passage they have gone through."

And the prayers for Jenna's salvation were answered. While Jenna still was a preschooler, as her parents were praying together with her at bedtime, she prayed so sweetly and sincerely, "Jesus forgive my sins and come into my heart."

*Dear Lord, keep us mindful of the Bible's teaching that without accepting Jesus none of us will be in heaven. Help us to pray for every one of our loved ones until they accept Jesus—so we can all be in heaven together. In Jesus' love, Amen.*

# TRAIN UP A CHILD

*Train up a child in the way he should go,*
*and when he is old he will not depart from it.*
Proverbs 22:6, NASB

hat about "train up a child in the way he should go, and when he is old he will not depart from it" (Prov. 22:6, NASB)? I have had many parents almost defensively say to me, "But I *have* trained up my child in the way he/she should go. So why isn't he/she living a Christian life?"

First that verse doesn't say that the child will never go through the "prodigal son" stage, rebelling against God and family. It says "when he is *old* he will not depart from it." That explains temporary "departings."

Also, I have been astounded at the lifestyle of some parents who honestly believed they had brought up their children "the way they should go." Examples in the home of self-centeredness instead of biblical caring for others, amassing treasure on earth instead of heaven, putting the body above the soul in priorities—all directed the child away from, instead of toward, God.

But there are Christian households in which children are trained to go God's way, and the children go wrong. Believing parents who have faithfully trained their children in the way they should go should not feel they are failures.

When parents have done the very best they could, but the children turn their backs on everything the parents hold dear, rebel at all that has been taught them, and pick friends that horrify the parents—it is time to reevaluate their children's actual relationship with Jesus. Of course, they may be just cutting the apron strings or trying their wings to find out who they are. But it is important to make sure your children actually have the new nature the Bible promises:

*For by these He has granted to us His precious and magnificent promises, in order that by them you might become partakers of the divine nature, having escaped the corruption that is in the world by lust* (2 Peter1:4, NASB, italics added).

*Dear Lord, help me to be alert to any loved ones whose lifestyles don't fit their words of commitment to Jesus. Keep me praying until they return to their commitment or receive Him as their Savior and Lord— no matter how long it takes.*
*In Jesus' name, Amen.*

# THE PRAYER FOR SALVATION

*God . . . desires all men to be saved
and to come to the knowledge of the truth.*
1 Timothy 2:3-4, NASB

es, the prayer for salvation is the most important prayer I, as their mother, prayed for Jan,
Nancy, and Kurt. I persisted, frequently agonized in
prayer, until I had listened to all of my three children
invite Jesus into their lives. It also was the most
important prayer my mother prayed for me.

I remember the family prayers that brought me to
Jesus. I was born into a family that knew nothing
about a personal relationship with Jesus. In fact, my
family knew little of Jesus Himself. But when my
mother trusted Jesus as her Savior when we children
were young, her first thought was for our salvation
too.

Nobody taught my mother to pray. There were no
prayer seminars and "how-to" books available to her.
She just listened to the older saints in Wednesday
night prayer meetings—and started to pray. And her
first prayers were for her children's and her husband's salvation. I was only nine years old when my
mother became a Christian, but it was my mother's

zeal for Jesus and the fervency of her prayer that brought results that very year.

Never question if it is right to pray for a family member's salvation. The Bible clearly says that "God . . . desires all men to be saved and to come to the knowledge of the truth" (1 Tim. 2:3-4, NASB). And again, "The Lord . . . is patient toward you, not wishing for any to perish but for all to come to repentance" (2 Peter 3:9, NASB).

Although Paul apparently never married, it was for his whole extended Jewish family that he said his "heart's desire and my prayer to God" was for their salvation (Rom. 10:1, NASB). And I have joined Paul in making this the number one prayer for my whole extended family too.

Have you made it your prayer for your family?

*Dear Lord, how grateful I am to You for a praying mother and sister—who didn't give up until I received Jesus as my personal Savior and Lord. My mother's greatest fear was that some of her loved ones would not be in heaven with her, but in a Christless eternity. Put that burden in all of us Christians.*
*In Jesus' name, Amen.*

# GOD'S METHOD OF TEACHING

*"If you abide in Me, and My words abide in you, ask whatever you wish, and it shall be done for you.*
John 15:7, NASB

uring the summer after Chris graduated from seminary, I had prayed and prayed for God to teach me how to be a pastor's wife. With trepidation in my heart at such a huge task looming in front of me, I sat at the feet of a pastor's wife I deeply respected, gleaning every speck of advice I could get. But God added His divine teaching.

I had been pregnant with Judy in 1952 when Chris went to his first church, but I certainly didn't understand that Judy's death at seven months was one of the ways He really was preparing me for the years ahead of that task.

It was over twenty-five years after Judy's death that I was on a California radio talk show and a woman called in from the East Coast. There wasn't a dry eye in the studio after she said to me, "I'm a Christian today because of watching you at my little sister's casket. When I was a little girl my baby sister died, and you and Pastor Chris came home from your vacation to have her funeral. Mrs. Chris, all you did at that mortuary was hold my mother in your arms and cry. And I remember saying to myself, 'If that's what a Christian is, I want to be one.' And I am."

It was March 23, 1971 while studying John 15:7 about Jesus' promise of astounding prayer power that I prayed, "Lord, I want that power in prayer. *Teach me and break me until I have it.*" Little did I realize that the way I would experience that power was in actually praying. And that it basically would be our family needs and difficulties that would keep this wife, mother, mother-in-law, and grandmother on her knees—wrestling, interceding, releasing.

Yes, I have experienced that tremendous power in prayer in a round-the-world prayer ministry. But I also have experienced the teaching, and the breaking, it has taken for God to answer that prayer for prayer power.

*Dear Heavenly Father, help me to see that You not only taught me but broke my heart through hard and sometimes devastating things—so that I could develop into the tender, understanding friend for others. And the prayer power I've learned has been from agonizing in prayer for loved ones' trials. Thanks, dear Father. In Jesus' name, Amen.*

## So Near, Yet So Far

*Nevertheless I am continually with Thee; Thou hast taken hold of my right hand.*

Psalm 73:23, NASB

The distance between you and your child's school, questionable social event, or just "out with the gang" can be just as devastating as if there were an ocean in between. But God's hand can reach children in those places too.

The sting of those early family separations was greatly reduced for us by our praying for our children. We sent our little ones out into a cruel world—not alone but with God. At our "front door praying" we prayed specifically about the bully on the playground, that day's difficult test, a tummy ache, or whatever was looming before them out there. Our hand could not hold theirs—and should not have. But we sent our children out with the invisible hand of God tightly holding theirs.

From the day our Jan entered kindergarten till when our last child, Kurt, graduated from high school, we never missed a day praying with each child at the door as they left. I'll admit there were times when our children were adolescents or teens that they rebelled, verbally, at having to wait at the door. And sometimes the prayers had to be just a few words "shot up to God on the run." But, looking back, I know how important those prayer times were—to them—and to us. They removed the fear and our possessiveness as God took over—when we couldn't. When we prayed for them, our children unknowingly had the same assurance as the psalmist in Psalm 73:23, "Nevertheless I am continually with Thee [God]; *Thou hast taken hold of my right hand*" (*NASB, italics added*).

*Dear Lord, it is so difficult to cut the apron strings of every age. But please help me, and all of us, to have the absolute assurance that, no matter how frightening the circumstances looming in front of them and us, You will be there! In Jesus' name, Amen.*

# THE SUPERNATURAL REASON FOR FAMILY PRAYER

*Be of sober spirit, be on the alert. Your adversary, the devil, prowls about like a roaring lion, seeking someone to devour. But resist him, firm in your faith, knowing that the same experiences of suffering are being accomplished by your brethren who are in the world.*

1 Peter 5:8-9, NASB

he only reason families need prayer is because there is a supernatural battle raging on earth, and human resources, wisdom, and power are not sufficient to win it.

All the things that make family prayer necessary—rebellion, dissension, unforgiveness, abuse, infidelity, sickness, pain, sorrow, and eternal damnation—were brought to earth by Satan. God's world was created perfect by Him, but when Satan tempted Eve to sin in the Garden of Eden, Adam and Eve fell. This opened the door for Satan to bring all this evil to Planet Earth. And he still is the source of all of it on earth—and thus in our families.

Since the source of all that plagues our families is supernatural, we need supernatural weapons to combat it, as Paul clearly emphasized:

*For though we walk in the flesh, we do not war according to the flesh, for the weapons of our war-*

*fare are not of the flesh, but divinely powerful for the destruction of fortresses (2 Cor. 10:3-4, NASB).*

The only One who can bring victory over all this evil that plagues our families is God. And the way we enlist His help for our families in this supernatural battle is prayer. When we pray, God enters the supernatural problem with His supernatural wisdom and power. So our supernatural weapon is prayer (see Eph. 2:18-20).

Now it is true that God is sovereign, and He does intervene in our families' problems as He chooses, but the only way we can enlist His help is through prayer. Prayer is the supernatural communication to a supernatural God who then supernaturally reaches down to our families and supernaturally brings the reconciliation, healing, peace, and love our family members need.

Are you enlisting God's power through prayer?

*Dear Lord Jesus, thank You that You defeated Satan once for all on the cross. We can't defeat him with human resources, so keep us praying—to bring Your divine victory and authority over him into our families and ourselves. In Your victorious name, Amen.*

# PONDERING OR PRAYING?

*Draw near to God, and He will draw near to you.*
James 4:8, NASB

uch of what we think is prayer actually is only pondering. Even when we are on our knees in our prayer closets, it is easy just to roll our own thoughts and our own answers around in our minds, not really including God at all. This is not prayer; it is only pondering.

My dictionary defines *ponder* like this: "To consider something deeply and thoroughly; to meditate over or upon, to weigh carefully in the mind; to consider thoughtfully; to reflect, cogitate, deliberate, ruminate." This is a healthy process as it helps us sort out whys, unravel perplexing puzzles, come to conclusions, and even put to rest hurtful events. But people frequently think they have prayed when they have spent time pondering. *Pondering is not prayer.* Only when we involve God in this process does it turn into prayer.

In the supernatural battle for our families, pondering is inadequate. It is powerless to change the family problem about which we are deliberating.

But when we include God, our pondering suddenly involves the omniscient, all-wise God of the universe. The God who never makes a mistake. The God who knows all the whys, all the outcomes, all the perfect He intends through everything that happens to our families. When God becomes personally involved in our pondering, there are accurate conclusions and correct attitudes in and for our families— supplied by a loving, caring, all-knowing God.

When our pondering turns to praying, we also have the divine input of the omnipotent, all-powerful God of heaven who has the power to intervene supernaturally in our family problems. And He also desires to supply us with all the power we need to cope with, handle, and solve our family needs.

Only when we include God in our ponderings are we praying.

Examine carefully what you have been calling your "prayer time." How much of it is really praying? Have you learned to address God deliberately—and then listen to His responses? Or are you basically just pondering? Make sure!

*Dear Father in heaven, when we involve You in our ponderings, we don't get only our own inadequate and frequently incorrect human answers, but wisdom from You—the omniscient, all-wise God of the universe. The God who never makes a mistake, knows all the whys, and all the outcomes You intend. How comforting; how sweet. Thanks, dear God! In Jesus' awesome name, Amen.*